The God
of Second Chances

The God
of Second Chances
A REAL LIFE STORY

BY KATHY ASHDOWN
WITH DR. SCOTT ASHDOWN

First Edition

ISBN-10: 0983130507

ISBN-13: 978 0983130505

http://www.grannyapplepublishing.com

GRANNY
APPLE
PUBLISHING

Contents

Dedication   ix
Acknowledgments   xi
Introduction   xiii

The Beginning Years

CHAPTER ONE   Mafia Meets McCoy   3
Skit   Mafia Meets McCoy   5

The Lonely Years

CHAPTER TWO   The Talented One   15

CHAPTER THREE   Passion   25
Song   I'll Sing to the World My Songs   27

The Growing Years

CHAPTER FOUR   The Year God Talked Back   31
Song   Happy Birthday Dear Jesus   36

CHAPTER FIVE   High School and Idols   39
Song   Let Go   42
Song   Ten Ways to Lose an Idol   44

CHAPTER SIX   College and Cavalcade   47
Song   Marching Orders   52

The Blessed Years

CHAPTER SEVEN   Elaine   57
Song   *The Ballad of Kathy and Elaine*   59

CHAPTER EIGHT   Home Again Home Again   61

The Painful Years

CHAPTER NINE   Kathy Gets Married   69
Skit   *Forgive and Forget*   73

CHAPTER TEN   The "C" Words   79
Song   *This One (Hopeless Face)*   86
Song   *Lizzytish*   88

CHAPTER ELEVEN   The "D" Word   91
Song   *Jesus' Face*   94

The Healing Years

CHAPTER TWELVE   God is My Husband   99
Song   *Ruth's Song*
                     (Lay Your Cloak Over Me)   107

CHAPTER THIRTEEN   Things Are Looking Up   109
Song   *Shout For Joy*   112

The Fruitful Years

CHAPTER FOURTEEN   Songs During the Fruitful Years 115
Song   *Looking Back*   116
Skit   *I Just Couldn't Say No*   117
Skong (Skit and Song) *What Will You Do About Jesus?*   119
Song   *Two Nights*   122

The Happy Years

| CHAPTER FIFTEEN | Scott and Kathy | 125 |
| Song | The IOU Song | 139 |

What Is a PJs Women's Conference?   141

About the Authors   143

Dedication

I dedicate this book, in loving memory, to my little sister, Elizabeth, who touched more lives for Christ than I can count; and to Sheryl Welch DeWitt, whose expertise in her field of psychology and counseling helped pave the way for light to shine into my family.

You are both in Heaven smiling down on me right now and I can't wait for the day when I will be able to see each of you again, face to face.

Acknowledgments

*T*o my Lord, for saving me and giving me a message of hope and the ability to share it with the world.

To my husband, for being just plain amazing, and loving me with unconditional love.

To my church, Grace Baptist, for allowing me to blossom.

To my family, for growing with me.

To my friends throughout the years who have stood by me through thick and thin.

To my publisher, Janet Verdeguer, without whom I could never have finished this book on time.

Introduction

*W*elcome, Reader!
I'm thrilled that you've decided to come along for the ride. Grab your comfy slippers and a hot cup of cocoa, and settle back for an amazing story about second chances. The best way to tackle this book is to have my CD, "The God of Second Chances," close by so that you can listen to each song as it is presented in the book.

Every song has a story behind it and I want you to discover each one just as I did within the context in which it was written. Because most of my songs are presented in chronological order, the styles change throughout the CD. I went through a Karen Carpenter stage when I was ten and a Keith Green stage when I was fourteen. Those styles clearly come through in my earlier music. But don't worry. Later on I wrote plenty of contemporary songs, too.

> *Every song has a story behind it and I want you to discover each one just as I did within the context in which it was written.*

Before we get going, I just want to say that even though I am a nobody, God is a big Somebody. Throughout the story, I reveal some pretty stupid mistakes I made along the way. As much as I hate to admit it, I am a sinner. (Thought I had better get that out of the way right off the bat.) But somehow, God found a way to use my mistakes and help others avoid the path I took.

Jeremiah wrote, *"Although our iniquities testify against us O Lord, act for Your name's sake." (Jeremiah 14:7)*

I have no credentials other than the fact that I have walked with Jesus for almost forty years. Scripture says, *"Now as they observed the confidence of Peter and John and understood that they were uneducated and untrained men, they were amazed and began to recognize them as having been with Jesus." (Acts 4:13)*

The end of that verse says "having been with Jesus." That's all I want you to see, that I, too, have been with Jesus who can make anyone's life interesting—even mine. Throughout history, the God of this Universe has been known to work miracles for the average Joe who strives to listen to His voice and who seeks to know Him more deeply. I didn't realize just how interesting my life with Him was until hearing from friends after my concerts. I often shared the circumstances behind the songs, and one evening a friend sat me down and said, "Kathy, your life was not normal! You need to write a book!"

I began writing down the stories that go with each song and soon it dawned on me that every story could be the title of a chapter in my life. I also began to see a few spiritual threads weaving throughout the tapestry of this colorful life:

First, God gave me a passion or, as the Bible calls it, a gift, at a very young age. The Bible says that He gives these gifts to His children and that He wants them to use these gifts to glorify Him and serve others.

Second, God used all of my life struggles to draw me closer to Him. Suffering is never in vain as it is a tool that God can use to draw us closer to Him. Suffering can strengthen us and mold our character to become more like His. Gold is refined by fire.

He is the God of second chances. No matter how badly you've messed up your life, it is never too late to start fresh and become all He intends you to be.

Third, He is the God of second chances. No matter how badly you've messed up your life, it is *never* too late to start fresh and become all He intends you to be.

These three principles run throughout my story. God has graciously allowed my concerts to blossom into a conference tour called "PJs Women's Conferences." The three principles I just mentioned are hidden in the conference title:

Passion: The gift that God gives to every woman to glorify Him and serve others

Jesus: The God of Second Chances

Suffering: A tool which God can use to draw us closer to Himself and make us more like Him

My prayer for you, dear Reader, is that my life story will bless you and encourage you and, at the same time, bring total glory to Jesus Christ. God bless you as you journey ahead.

—Kathy Ashdown

The Beginning Years

Chapter One: Mafia Meets McCoy

*M*y mom and dad met in Brooklyn and theirs was a love at first sight. My dad's family was in the mafia; in fact, one of my dad's uncles was nicknamed "Jimmy the Bomber." My mom's family came from a long line of McCoys. Remember the famous feud of the Hatfields and the McCoys? What a pair, huh?

My parents, Joe and Joan
Catuara, on their honeymoon.

Both my parents brought their own baggage into the marriage and I'm not talking about violin cases or shotgun holsters. Their relationship worked well, because they had very similar

Mom and Dad were definitely equally yoked!

backgrounds and were just feisty enough for each other! Well, believe it or not, this fiery Irish girl and this staunch Italian boy met, fell in love, and married in the Catholic Church. Then they did the unthinkable and stayed happily married for more than fifty years.

A few years ago, my brothers, sisters, and I gave my parents a 50th wedding anniversary party. My job was to interview them separately about how they met. When I cornered them individually with their morning coffee in hand, they both related the same exact story. It was so hilarious I decided to write a poem about it. Later that morning while my sisters and I indulged ourselves in a "group pedicure," all voices faded away as I sat there writing on a napkin.

Before I knew it, my toes were gorgeous and the poem was complete!

This poem is actually the first song on my CD and the drama team that travels with me to the PJs Conferences performs it as a skit. You can view some funny photos of the skit on my website at www.KathyAshdown.com.

Okay. Got your cup of coffee and your CD player ready? Enjoy.

Track#1: MAFIA MEETS McCOY

The month was November of '52.
Joe worked at Wittlesee and Joan worked there, too.
She was 20 and he 24
When he wandered up to the 14th floor.

He asked an employee, "Who is that over there?
The skinny secretary with the dark brown hair.
Is she married? Boyfriend? Is she going steady?"
"No," said the girl. "Her name is Joan Edde."

"Introduce me!" he said as he spiffed up his suit.
"I want to ask her out. I think she's cute."
They met and they talked. "Ask her now!" the guy said.
But whenever he tried to his ears would turn red.

Joe glanced at his watch. It was 4:04.
He opted to asking her for coffee next door.
She smiled and said, "You're a little too late.
I've already had my half-hour break."

The next day at exactly 3:04
Joe invited her again to coffee next door.
She smiled and said, "You're a little too late.
I've already had my half-hour break."

The next day at exactly 2:04
Joe invited her again to coffee next door.
She smiled and said, "You're a little too late.
I've already had my half-hour break."

> *Joe started to leave, but then he stopped.*
> *"Do you want to go out with me or not?"*
> *She smiled and said with a tilt of her head,*
> *"Joe, I would love to, but I plan ahead.*
> *Ask me today for tomorrow instead."*

The following day at 1:04
He and Joan Edde had coffee next door.
"Do you like bowling?" he finally said.
Then both of his ears turned bright, bright red.

> *The date was set and bowling the plan.*
> *But Joe needed help so he called Cousin Anne.*
> *"Anne!" he said with a sigh on the phone.*
> *"Will you come, too? I can't do this alone!"*

"Why?" she said. "You're a wonderful man."
"You'll win her over. I know you can!"
"I can't! There's a glitch and it's serious!" he said.
"Every time I get near her my ears turn bright red!"

> *On the night of the date, he arrived in his car.*
> *Joe said, "You look great...how stylish you are!"*
> *She was just about to say something sweet,*
> *When she saw Cousin Anne nestled in the front seat.*

Joan wasn't the only one suffering from shock.
You see, Joe was Italian and Joan was not.
Anne was not happy and she made a fuss.
She said in Italian, "She's not one of us!"

The Irish don't understand Italians as a rule.
But this Irish girl had aced Italian in school.
She acted as if it was all fine and dandy,
Knowing her secret would come in real handy.

She survived Cousin Anne and at the end of the night
Joe asked her out again and she said she might.
He needed a date for an upcoming dance.
She said, "Lose Cousin Anne and you might have a chance!"

The night of the dance, he alone came to call.
He stood nervously at the door…red ears and all.
Then all of a sudden, he let go all his fears,
When she said, "You look handsome…
Especially your ears!"
And that's what she said for the next 50 years.

Both of my parents' fathers were—how can I say this?—scoundrels. My dad's father was one of those rare mafia members who did not value family. He gave his wife and children no money to live on, but would buy fancy suits and hats to go out on the town. At night, he returned home drunk and beat up my grandma and anyone who tried to stop him. My grandfather wouldn't let her work. As soon as her kids were old enough, they each found jobs and gave all of their money to Grandma so that she could run the household. It was no surprise that they loved their mother dearly and hated their father deeply.

My dad moved his mother and all of his eight brothers and sisters to a new location three times trying to lose their father. Unfortunately, my grandfather found them twice and beat the holy cannoli out of them. Finally, the third time did the trick and my grandfather never showed up again. The family thought he might have had an "accident." Enough said. Obviously, my dad had no male role model to look up to or emulate.

My mom's father abandoned his wife and children when my mom was very young. Though she didn't know him well, my mom hated her father for leaving. Later on, she had to quit high school in order to help support the family. Just like my dad, my mom loved her mother dearly.

My grandmother had a club foot and couldn't get around easily. Her bedroom was right off the kitchen near the back door. When the kids came home too late, my grandmother would lock the front door so that they had to pass through the kitchen to get into the house. She would leave her bedroom door opened and, as they snuck by hoping not to wake her, she would throw her big orthopedic shoe at them. My mom said that shoe looked like a brick and it felt like a shot-put disk upside the head. Mom got wise, though, and started sending her friends in first.

My parents had a lot in common: both lacked a father figure; both worked very hard from a young age, and both gave all of their money to their mothers.

My dad adored my mother and treated her like a queen. He hated New York and wanted to get as far away from it as possible, so he moved with my mother to sunny California and never looked back. The sunshine must have done them some good because they proceeded to have eight children.

The prevailing philosophy in our household growing up seemed to be that my dad was the king and we were nobody. He would jokingly say, "I'm the king and you're nobody." But it didn't seem like a joke to us because we believed him.

I want to stop a minute and tell you that my parents and most of my brothers and sisters have been through counseling. Our relationships are much different now than they were back then, so keep that in mind as I write about life in those early days. For instance, Dad has since mellowed and learned better ways of relating to his children.

During my childhood, however, I felt like a little ant who was only alive to serve my father. His discipline style was severe. Sometimes, if we walked by him while he was reading the paper, he would hit us and mumble, "That was for yesterday when you slammed the door." Or, "That was for last week when you rolled your eyes at your mother." I was terrified to walk past him for fear I'd get bopped.

I know my parents loved me, but I don't ever remember them saying the actual words "I love you." Once in high school, my friend Deanna and I were leaving her house when her mother called out from the kitchen, "Bye, Sweetie, I love you!" Deanna hollered back, "Love you too, Mom!" I marveled at that for days.

Can you imagine never hearing those words? I think my parents just assumed we knew they loved us. After all, they provided for us, protected us from harm, took us on family vacations, and spent thousands of dollars on Christmas gifts to make sure we had a better Christmas than they did growing up. My mom changed diapers for thirty years and cooked 10,590 meals. My parents made good moral decisions for us by providing a private Catholic School education. Yet, the words I longed to hear were never said.

My dad was very, very intelligent and worked in the aerospace industry on secret government projects. He also loved music and most nights would sit on the couch next to the stereo listening to his classical music with big old earphones on his head. I somehow figured out that it was talent and brains that could elevate me from ant status to human status. If you had been a fly on our wall, you would have seen that our dinner conversations were made up of one fact after another flying across the table. The voices that were respected and listened to were the ones with the latest, most accurate statistics. No feeling words ever flew across that table.

My mom had her hands full running such a large household and, at the same time, finishing up her education. She was organized and stayed on top of things. She was funny and outgoing, and I thought she was the most beautiful mom in the world. I loved it when she came to visit my classroom because kids would come up to me and say, "Wow, your mom is so pretty!" I wanted her all to myself but never really got a lot of one-on-one time with her.

My mom didn't tuck us in at night or read bedtime stories. But, when we were sick, she would take us to the doctor, and afterwards treat the patient to lunch at the Harvey House. I loved that! It was almost worth being sick just to spend alone time with her. When she went grocery shopping, one of us went along to help and was rewarded with a candy bar. But that candy bar meant nothing to me compared to the privilege of being alone with her.

Mom wasn't a hugger. The only physical form of affection I can remember was when she sat next to me at the dinner table and she would place her arm on the back of my chair and gently scratch my back. I lived for those tender back scratches!

My mother's form of discipline was to raise her hands dramatically in the air and holler, "Lord, give me patience with this child!" and then give me the silent treatment. I'm pretty sure she only used this method of discipline on me. The rest of the kids got a hairbrush to the behind.

Even though on the outside my mom looked like she had it all together, she was very nervous on the inside. Mom recently told me that it was very important to her, back then, that the family appear perfect to anyone looking in from the outside. She thought that if the family didn't appear this way, it somehow reflected on her. But keeping up this facade exhausted her. I don't know how she did it.

When my oldest brother turned twelve, my dad decided it was time to take us all to New York to meet the relatives. My mom was pregnant with her seventh child and nervous about taking so many kids and toddlers on a plane flight. She expressed her concerns to our neighbor who proceeded to give her Valium for the trip. My mom had never taken Valium before. She was a "take two aspirins and go to bed" kind of gal. On the way to the airport, she popped two of those little blue pills, thinking, "Two are probably better than one." When we got to the L.A. Airport, my dad said, "Joan, stay here with the kids while I check in the luggage."

After about half an hour my dad returned to find my mom sitting alone with a dopey look on her face. "Uh…Joan, where are the kids?" She smiled and said, "What kids?" We were wandering all over the airport without a care in the world. I don't recall my mom ever taking Valium again.

We had no idea how they resolved any conflicts because whenever there was a disagreement, they would walk to Bob's Big Boy restaurant and "discuss it" there....

My siblings and I never saw my parents fight. We had no idea how they resolved any conflicts because whenever there was a disagreement, they would walk to Bob's Big Boy restaurant and "discuss it" there. Consequently, none of us learned how to handle conflict. Instead, we learned how to avoid it.

My mom's fear of how we appeared coupled with my dad's totalitarian kingship resulted in the two of them making most of their children's decisions for them. Dad and Mom decided how we wore our hair, the décor of our rooms, and what we ate for lunch.

Afraid I might burn the meal, my mother never let me cook dinner for the family. I remember after years of asking her if I could pour Bugles into a bowl for Christmas guests, she finally announced, "I think you're old enough." My hands shook as this monumental task was entrusted to me. To this day, I still get a little

Airport fiasco

nervous pouring milk for fear I might spill it. Every year I asked my dad if I could help put up the Christmas tree lights, but he said they were too fragile. I never did learn how to do that. At eighteen years old, we were sent out into the world with very little decision-making skills and, I can tell you, I made some pretty bad decisions later on.

My parents, unlike many others, have since learned to dialog with me about these issues and have changed their parenting style in many positive ways. After a very significant "marriage encounter" weekend, my dad realized that we needed to hear the words "I love you." He met with each of us individually, held our hands, looked us squarely in the eyes, and finally said those words I longed to hear. Today, my mom often says on the phone, "Love you, Gal!" They both have come a long way in the communication department.

The Lonely Years

Chapter Two: The Talented One

efore I start this chapter, I want to apologize for talking so much about myself. Please forgive me! God had not yet entered my life, and during these early years, it was pretty much all about me. You need to know what I was like in order to see the big job God had ahead of Him.

Okay, here we go. That's me, Kathleen, the third child born into the Catuara family. And no, I will not give you the date of my birth. (A woman has to have some secrets, you know!) But I will, however, tell you my weight…at birth, that is.

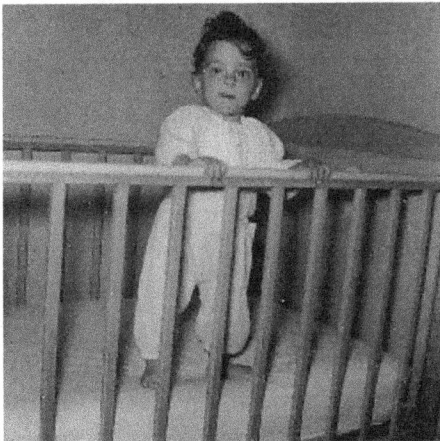

Kathy as an infant trying to market a new hairstyle

Born a "preemie," I weighed in at only two-and-a-half pounds. My dad said he held me in the palm of his hand and fed me with a doll bottle. I'm told that after one of those nice feedings I was placed on my tummy in the warm incubator with hopes of encouraging a few burps. Instead, I lifted up my head straining to look all around me. The nurse was shocked and said to my mother, "This one is going to be a handful. You'd better get ready!" Actually, I think it was just a reaction to good food. I still get excited over a good meal!

When I was about three-and-a-half years old, my older siblings, Joey and Joanie, went off to school leaving me at home with my mom and baby sister, Maureen. Our home had a nice big family room with a TV and a piano in it. One morning, while we were watching TV, my mom stepped out of the room for a minute. Suddenly, she heard someone playing the piano to the tune of the commercials. She quickly ran back for fear someone was in the house. No one was there except me and Maureen looking up at her in bewilderment.

At the next commercial, she slipped behind the doorway and slowly peeked around the corner. This time she saw me walk over to the piano, reach up and begin to play the tune I was hearing on TV. She couldn't believe her eyes.

My mom immediately tried to find a piano teacher but no one would take a three-year-old. After many rejections, she came up with an idea and called a teacher named Mrs. Wolfe, telling her she had three children who wanted lessons: Joey, Joanie and Kathleen. What teacher in their right mind wouldn't jump at the chance to get three new students all in one shot? But when my mom told her my age, Mrs. Wolfe agreed to teach the older two children but not me. Undaunted, my mother took the phone and me over to the piano and made her listen to me play along with several commercials.

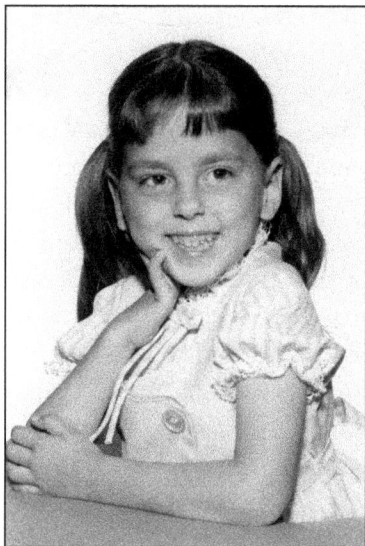

Kathy at three years old

Mrs. Wolfe exclaimed on the other end of the phone, "That is amazing! She is a child prodigy! I would be delighted to take her as a student." Thus I was dubbed, "The Talented One" in the family. Ant status: gone.

At age four, I performed in my first recital. Try to imagine how Joey and Joanie felt. It was not easy for them to constantly hear how talented I was and eventually they quit taking lessons. My parents' open praise of me caused an unspoken club to form at my house called the "Not Liking Kathleen" club. From here on in I'm going to refer to this club as the "IHK" club for short, meaning "I Hate Kathleen." If you asked them now, my sisters and brothers would probably not admit that they actually hated me, but it sure felt like they did. Years later, in counseling, it came out that many of them were jealous of the attention I received.

The IHK club gained momentum as the family grew in size.

First Recital

The kids were assigned KP duty after dinner, but many times my mom would say, "Kathleen, go practice your piano." This announcement did not thrill my siblings or me. Practicing was torture. It was lonely. The family room was right next to the kitchen and I could hear my brothers and sisters having fun talking, laughing, and towel whipping each other. I would much rather have joined them.

The final blow which pretty much solidified, incorporated and patented the IHK club occurred when my parents found out I had Attention Deficit Disorder, or ADD. They opted not to put me on medication because, at that time, not enough studies had been completed to prove the long-term effects of Ritalin.

The doctor sat my parents down and said, "Listen, just give her lots of attention and make sure she gets all of her energy out before bedtime. Let her swim or something."

Now, that went over real well with my sisters and brothers: "Time for bed, kids! Kathleen, you get to swim." Unlike Joseph in the Bible, my sisters and brothers could not sell me into slavery (although they would have liked to). Instead, they did the next best thing—they completely and utterly ignored me.

I was a pretty happy kid until I was about six years old when I really started feeling the loneliness caused by my siblings ignoring me. In a family of ten the atmosphere was filled with what I like to call "hubbub." But the hubbub never seemed to invite me in. To make matters even worse, I was dubbed "The Pretty One."

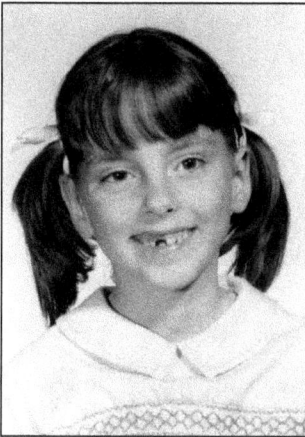

A face only a mother could love

It just wasn't true. Come on now, isn't that a face only a mother could love? I think all of my sisters are beautiful.

Nevertheless, "Pretty" was added to the list of reasons why my siblings shunned me.

For years, my family held sacred a weekly dinner we called, "The Wednesday Night Spaghetti Night." Ever since I can remember, without exception, spaghetti was always served on Wednesday nights. Even after marriage and kids, we still showed up for Wednesday night dinner.

Just as a fun side note, my mom refused to buy a pot big enough to properly cook all the pasta needed. Instead she cooked pasta for ten people in a medium-sized pot which caused the spaghetti to turn out sticky. The cooked spaghetti looked like a giant webbed football on a platter.

For years we pleaded, "Ma! Get a bigger pot!" but to no avail. Finally, one night when she placed the platter on the dinner table, my brother, Chris, said, "Mom, would you please cut me an end piece?"

The Catuaras, from top left, clockwise: Joanie, Adrienne, Bobby, Joey, Maureen, Chris, Kathleen, Liz, Dad, Mom.

Oh, we tried not to laugh. We tried *so* hard not to laugh. But there we were, shoulders shaking, tears rolling, snorting to hold it in. But we just couldn't do it. We started laughing so hard we couldn't stop. She bought a bigger pot.

I bring up spaghetti night because in my early twenties, I invited a friend over for dinner on a Wednesday night. Afterwards, my family subjected him to the worst form of torture known to man: home movies. After the long ordeal was over, we turned the lights back on and I noticed that my friend was crying. I thought, "Uh oh, it was worse than I thought. We brought him to tears."

He pulled me aside and said, "Kathy, I'm crying because in every movie the kids are over here playing together and you are over there alone. It's the saddest thing I've ever seen. You didn't even try to join in. How did you cope?"

"Well," I answered, "at night while I was swimming alone to work off my energy, I would float on my back and talk to God."

You see, I was Catholic, so I had learned about God. When I was lonely and desperate for someone to talk to, I would imagine He spoke to me through the trees that hung over our pool. I would ask Him a question and it seemed to me that the wind would shake the leaves wildly for a "yes" answer and gently for a "no" answer. I thought for sure it was God because the wind would blow immediately after I asked the question. Was it my imagination or was it Him wooing me? I think God was using my loneliness to draw me to Him.

In an effort to find someone to talk to, I looked for friendship outside my family. Once, I thought I had found a friend in a neighbor girl until she started locking me in her shed and sticking sticks down my underwear. She would leave me there for hours warning me that, if I took them out, I would be sorry. She was a big girl and threatened to beat me up if I ever told anyone. I was so scared of her I never told a soul until she moved away.

I remember my first day of school like it was yesterday. I was so excited because going to school meant getting away from that bully girl and having someone to talk to. My hopes were high; I was going to try very hard to blend in and not be an outcast.

I went to a Catholic school with all the trimmings— uniforms, nuns and mass in the mornings. The nuns had their own way of disciplining back then, which, of course, they could never get away with today. They were highly respected and our parents would say, "Oh yes, Sister Benigna! Whatever you say, Sister Benigna."

Well, one nun decided that the only way to keep this hyperactive child still was to tie me to my desk with a belt. Now that's a great way to blend in! The moment that belt went around me I kissed any hopes of friendships goodbye. I was labeled the weird kid and nobody would sit with me at lunch.

Something in me just snapped at that point. No amount of favor from my parents could make up for the loneliness I was feeling. I don't know if I just didn't want anyone at school to know I was being shunned or that I refused to face rejection since I already faced it at home every day, but at lunch time I started going into the bathroom and eating my lunch in the stall. If any students came in I would lift my feet up so no one knew I was there.

...I started going into the bathroom and eating my lunch in the stall. If any students came in I would lift my feet up so no one knew I was there....

I did this for eight years. I ate alone in that stall day after day, waiting for the bell to ring so that nobody would know I had no friends. One year, a girl named Donna Irwin decided to be my friend, but that was short lived. She moved to another school and it was back to the bathroom again. My question now is: how is it that no teacher ever realized this? Did they think I had stomach problems or something? Running diarrhea for eight years? I started to believe I really was weird.

In one way, I *was* weird. Any praise I received at home was strictly in proportion to how well I performed, so that became my lifeline. Whenever I met someone for the first time I pretty much said, "Hi, my name is Kathleen, I play the piano and I'm a child prodigy. Wanna hear me? Here I go."

I asked the nuns every day if I could play for the class. I think I was reaching out for some sense of self worth. I figured it worked at home with my parents so maybe it would work at school. Well, it totally backfired because now, besides being called weird, I was also labeled a show-off. And no one likes a show-off.

For a while, my mom's friend, Shirley, lived across the street from us. Shirley had a daughter my age named Margie who was a ballerina and, for some reason, liked me. I don't know why she liked me, but she did. What would I have done without Margie? Then one day her family moved across town and I didn't get to see her as much after that.

Mo is happily playing as Adrienne listens.

I was in fifth grade when my little sister, Maureen, got a guitar for Christmas. A week before that my mom sat me down and explained to me that Mo (that was her nickname) had been acting out lately. My mother thought Mo's problem stemmed from the fact that she didn't get to learn an instrument like her older brothers and sisters had. I specifically remember my mom warning me not to touch that guitar because it was going to be "Mo's instrument" in the hopes it would make her feel like she had a talent. Isn't it interesting how parents pigeonhole us sometimes? I was okay with that until Mo opened that shiny new guitar on Christmas morning. Look at her face in the photo—how happy she was! My face?—not so happy. The green-eyed monster crept in and whispered to me, "Mo's not the musician in this family. You are!"

Mo and I shared a bedroom and she decided to keep her guitar under her bed. So...here's what I did. I faked a stomach ache one day and while everyone was at school, I took that guitar out of the case and strummed it. It was calling to me: "Come and play me!

It's okay if no one knows you can play." (Doesn't that sound like the forbidden fruit conversation?)

I *loved* playing that guitar! I started sneaking it out every chance I had. I was alone so much that it felt like a good friend. I kept up this secret love affair for months, always waiting until everyone was gone before I pulled it out from under my sister's bed. I guess you could call me a closet guitarist.

You need to understand something about Mo. She had a mouth on her that could cut you to pieces. She was smart, witty and quick, but she was also hurting inside. Because Mo was often overlooked in our family system, her sharp tongue was the only way she knew how to be heard. Mo remembers this about herself. I'm not saying anything she wouldn't tell you.

Kathy is definitely not happy.

Our beds were across from each other and she would torment me, late at night, whispering, "You know, Kathleen, you were adopted." She could keep this going for weeks saying, "Mom and Dad don't really love you. You're actually a pygmy. Don't you wonder why you get so tan in the summer? Your real parents didn't want you."

Mo could drive anyone to the brink of insanity. I remember one night, around midnight, my parents heard screaming and came running into the kitchen to find me kneeling over Mo with a kitchen knife. I was screaming, "Take it back! Take it back! I am *not* a pygmy!" I had no intention of actually doing her any harm, but it worked. She took it back.

A few months after this little incident, Mo was tormenting me again. Having no kitchen utensils nearby, I did the next best thing. Knowing these words would just kill her, I yelled, "And I've been playing your guitar for months and I learned the whole book and I wrote a song and you're only on page ten!"

Doesn't that sound like Joseph bragging about his dreams? If you could have seen her face, a knife would have been less painful. I got in so much trouble. Big—no, *huge*—repercussions ensued and I landed in more hot water over this than I did over the knife incident!

As a result, Mo and I were split up and no longer shared a bedroom. I was relocated to a bedroom on the opposite side of the house, and was not allowed in her room or even the bathroom next to it. There was no discussion, no conflict resolution, no "Let's work this out," just separation. And, of course, the guitar went with her.

I decided then to save up my money and buy my own guitar which is exactly what I did! No one was going to tell me what instrument I could and couldn't play. I was the musician in the family, remember? Then to really get my parents' goat, I quit piano lessons; I just wouldn't practice anymore. I can still hear my dad saying, "We spent thousands of dollars on you all these years!" In my mind I silently retorted, "Guitar is my instrument now."

Chapter Three: Passion

Remember in my rampage to hurt Mo I told her I had written a song? Well, the truth was that I actually *had* written a song. Partly in rebellion towards my parents, I titled it, "I'll Sing to the World My Songs." It is number two on the CD. But before you listen to it, I want to say a little something about passion. Passion is the first word in the acrostic PJs which appears in the title of our women's conferences.

P stands for: Passion, every woman's gift
J stands for: Jesus is the God of second chances
S is for: Suffering, God's tool to draw us closer to Him

These topics are woven throughout a PJs Conference weekend like threads in a tapestry. I want to park on Passion for a minute.

What's eerie about the song I wrote was that at ten years old there was no way that I could have seen ahead to what God had planned for me. Though not a Christian song, it was like a prophecy. The passion was there. God gives every one of His children a unique and special gift. This passion, as I like to call it, is meant to be used for His glory, and usually reveals itself at a young age. Think back on your childhood. Was there something you loved to do? Was there something you were good at? I know life happens. You have to make a living. You have a family. But I still believe that we are each stewards of a gift from Him and we will be held accountable if we ignore it.

I don't mean to sound all doom and gloom. It's just that using your gift is what God knows will make you joyful, alive, and passionate, because He built you to be the conduit of that particular gift. I smile when women say to me, "I would love to serve Him in such and such a ministry but it would be way too much fun. Can that be from God? I'd better check with Him."

Honey, He was probably the one who put the idea in your head in the first place! Like Peter said, *"As each one has received a special gift, employ it in serving one another as good stewards of the manifold grace of God" (1 Peter 4:10).*

I truly believe that when we stand before the Lord He is going to say something like: "Susie, I gave you a passion for cooking. How did you use that to glorify me?" "Joan, I gave you a passion for teaching. How did you use that to serve me?" The operative word here is *passion*. What were you passionate about as a child? Think back.

> ***...It has to be Him leading you and Him giving you the energy to pull it off....***

One of the goals at the PJs Conference is to try to help women discern their passion. Together, we brainstorm ways to use their gifts within their sphere of influence. It's never too late to rekindle your gift. Maybe you are a stay-at-home mom with kids in diapers. You can still use your gifts to bless and encourage your kids, and at the same time enjoy being what God created you to be.

If you have a minute, take a piece of paper and, on one side, write down an activity you absolutely loved doing as a child. That could very well be your gift. On the other side, write down the obstacles that prevent you from executing that gift right now. Pray about these obstacles and ask the Lord to remove them or ask Him to show you how to work through them. By the way, as many times as you read in God's word to "use your gifts," it also says to serve "in the strength which God supplies." That's crucial. It has to be Him leading you and Him giving you the energy to pull it off. Your sphere of service may be limited to your own family right now but I can guarantee *you* have a gift that will bless them and glorify the Lord.

I'm embarrassed to tell you this, but I argued with God for ten years about developing the PJs Conferences. I said, "You got the wrong gal, God." But you know what? He didn't let up on me. My prayer is that He won't let up on you either.

Track#2: I'LL SING TO THE WORLD MY SONGS

Chorus
I'll sing to the world my songs,
I'll sing to the world my songs.

Verse 1
I'll sing to all people whether good or bad.
I'll make the sad happy and the happy sad
With my songs...I'll sing my songs.

Chorus
I'll sing to the world my songs,
I'll sing to the world my songs.

Verse 2
All the children will stop their trikes and bikes
When I warm their hearts with the songs they like.
My songs...they'll like my songs.

Chorus
I'll sing to the world my songs,
I'll sing to the world my songs.

Verse 3
The young and old will all draw near.
It won't be long till they all hear
My songs...you'll hear
My songs,
My songs,
My songs.

The Growing Years

Chapter Four:
The Year God Talked Back

I was thirteen years old when one of the nuns came to me and asked if I would be willing to teach guitar lessons after school...for money!

Obviously my answer was a resounding "yes." Her reason was that the church had a "guitar choir" that played at the 11:00 am mass every Sunday. Lots of kids wanted to learn guitar just so they could be in that choir. By the end of the year, I was teaching thirty students a week who all played on Sundays. The guitar choir was really cool and a bit funky. Imagine thirty guitars up in the choir loft accompanying thirty voices. One guitar is beautiful enough, but thirty acoustic guitars all playing at the same time? I've never heard anything like it since. The 11:00 am service was packed every Sunday; it had become the most popular Catholic service in the city.

Why am I telling you this? Because when the director got married, she asked me to take over directing the choir. I was only fourteen years old, but I jumped at the chance. As soon as I accepted, something drastically changed; I became popular. Because of being visible every Sunday and receiving a lot of attention and notoriety, boys started noticing me. This instant popularity also got me an "in" with the popular kids. Unfortunately, the popular kids were smokers, druggies and promiscuous girls. But for the first time since kindergarten...I was not eating lunch alone in the bathroom.

My behavior took a turn for the worse when I hung out with the "in" crowd, especially the boys. Yet I would show up every Sunday, looking sweet and innocent, leading that guitar choir. My parents decided to send me to an all girls Catholic High School, called Pomona Catholic, which students referred to as P.C. for Prison Camp. The worst part about P.C. was that the school had no music program and no men—the two things I clung to for dear life. I will hereby label my two vices "M & M," which stands for music and men. The thought of going to a school with neither of these lifelines made me panic and so I did what most children dream of doing at some point in their childhood—I ran away from home.

I didn't go far though. I stuffed my clothes in my guitar case and moved into my friend Mary's motor home, conveniently parked in her backyard. No one knew I was there except for Mary and I was livin' large! She snuck food out to me every night and, boy, could her mom cook! I could've stayed there indefinitely but the police finally cracked her. When my parents came to retrieve me they were more hurt than mad. I had never seen them so scared. They made a deal with me that seemed like a good compromise.

My parents really believed I would like P.C., so they decided to enroll me for one year. If I didn't like it, they told me, I could switch over to Chaffey High School, which boasted an award-winning music program and about 1,500 boys. Tough decision, huh? I counted the days at P.C. and couldn't wait for the year to end. I was miserable every step of the way and I let my parents and everyone else know it.

One of the members of my guitar choir could see how miserable I was. Her name was Julie Robson and she was convinced I needed the Lord. She started asking me to go with her to a Monday night Bible study at a Catholic church in the rich part of town. I had no interest in this at all, but she kept bugging me

Sunday after Sunday, saying, "Come with me tomorrow night! You'll love it!" Julie told me that the Bible study teacher was a young, pretty, Italian hippie who was really cool. Diane Santarelli was her name and she didn't shave her legs (that meant hippie in those days). Finally, Julie got smart and said, "By the way, Kathy, the *cutest* guys go there!" Well, that was all it took. I was wasting away in that all-girls school and needed to meet some guys to perk me up.

I went with Julie the next Monday night and she was right. There were so many good looking guys that I struggled to pay attention to the hippie girl...until her fiancée, Roger Ingolia, got up to speak. He was called the Italian Stallion and was he ever! Roger was tall, dark and handsome and I was in *love* (not knowing at the time that he and Diane were engaged). As I was drooling over Roger, he started to tell a story, and it was at that precise moment that my life changed forever—that was the moment when God entered.

Roger said, "I was driving down the mountain in my van with my earphones on and the Lord was speaking to my heart. He was just speaking to my heart." As soon as Roger said this, everything seemed to fade away and my heart started beating wildly. My face got beet red and I said to myself: "God talks back...*God talks back*??? All these years I've been talking to Him through the trees and it's earphones He uses? I gotta get me a pair of those earphones!" So, after the study I went right up and asked Roger where I could buy a pair of those earphones. Well, he led me to the Lord right there and then.

Now, I knew Jesus was my Savior, I saw Him hanging on the cross every Sunday at mass. But He wasn't my Lord, which means He wasn't in charge of my life—I was.

Roger taught me a new word; well, it was new to me. The word was "will." Remember when Jesus said, "Not my will but Thine be done?" I said those words for years in church but never knew what they meant. Roger explained I was to do the Lord's "will" every day.

That concept was totally foreign to me. "How do I know what His will is for me?" I asked.

"Well," Roger said, "When you ask Him to be the Lord of your life, He gives you His words to instruct you and guide you. Those words are right here in the Bible."

I stared down at the big red Bible in Roger's hand. "What if I don't understand it?" I asked.

Roger replied, "He also gives you His Holy Spirit that dwells inside you and helps you understand His words. The Holy Spirit gives you the power to carry out God's will."

Frankly, I was thrilled I wouldn't have to talk to those trees anymore. I had lots of questions for Roger and Diane so I stayed there very late getting answers.

Roger and Diane Ingolia

When I got home, I ran in the door, woke up my parents and held up the big red Bible that Roger had given me. "Mom, Dad, it's about a personal relationship! It's not about sitting in the pew every Sunday. God speaks to us through this Bible! He has a plan and He wants us to follow it. God wants to speak to us every day!"

Looking back now, the fact that I woke my parents from a sound sleep probably didn't help much, but I naively waited for them to say: "Really? Tell us all about it." Instead, I'll never forget this picture. My mom, in curlers and a pink robe, started pacing the floor, waving her hands dramatically in the air and wailing: "Satan has pulled her off the beaten path! Satan has pulled her off the beaten path!" The whole family was up by now and they started mumbling "Jesus freak," or words to that effect. So, to add to my labels of "talented," and "the pretty one," I was now also a "Jesus freak." Just pound another nail in my coffin.

You know what though? It didn't matter. I was so excited about this new relationship that nothing else mattered. I had real joy for the first time in my life. By some strange miracle, my parents let me continue going to that Bible study. Maybe they thought it was just a phase. Some phase! I went to that study for the next ten years. It would have been very easy for my dad to forbid me to go, but God intervened knowing it had to be a Catholic study. God planned it and I wasn't even looking. He knew how to lure me and I am so thankful He did.

God also replaced my old friends with new ones. He does that you know. I made lifelong Christian friends and the "in" girls I had been hanging out with just drifted away. Some of those kids ended up having really sad lives—that could have been me. It would have been me if God hadn't nudged Julie to bug me.

One of the brand new Christian friends I made was a spunky, blonde, Italian girl

Denise DeMarco

named Denise DeMarco. God kept sending Italians my way. (Don't you just love it?) If you've ever watched the TV series "Lost," then you know the power of the word "constant." When it comes to friendships, Denise is my constant. We've been friends for so many years, we are more like sisters. You'll hear more about her later.

Remember that song, "I've got that joy, joy, joy, joy down in my heart?" Well, that was me. God meets every new Christian at their point of need; mine was loneliness and I couldn't imagine ever feeling alone again. Christmas came shortly after I asked Jesus into my heart, and it was then that I wrote my next song. I was fifteen and this song was very different from the first one. This time I really had something substantial to say.

Every Christmas Eve, I would sneak into the bathroom after my parents went to bed and stay awake there all night. I was too excited to sleep, plus I wasn't allowed to swim because of Santa coming. I would sit on the edge of the tub and play my guitar and draw pictures. (What is it with me and bathrooms?) Anyway, my little sisters and brothers would come in and ask me to draw Santa or a Christmas tree, and we would quietly sing Christmas Carols until sun-up. My parents, to this day, do not know about that Christmas ritual (but I guess they will after reading this).

On that special Christmas Eve it dawned on me, "Wow, this is the first Christmas I really know You, Lord. You are my best friend, it's Your birthday, and I didn't even get you a present." I decided right there on the edge of the bathtub to write a birthday song for Him. It's song number three on the CD.

Track#3: HAPPY BIRTHDAY DEAR JESUS

Verse 1
Happy birthday dear Jesus, Happy Birthday this morn.
I'd like to give to you a gift
You gave to me when I was born.
Still in my mother's womb when music filled the room,
It found its way to tiny ears.
It hasn't left me all these years.

Oh, please receive my gift this Christmas morn.
I'm giving you my song on Christmas morn.

Verse 2
Happy birthday dear Jesus, Happy birthday this morn.
I'd like to give to you the gift
You gave the day I was reborn.
Into my darkened mind you let your love light shine.
It found its way into my heart,
A brand new life a brand new start.
Oh, please receive my gift this Christmas morn.
I'm giving you my life on Christmas morn.

Verse 3
Happy birthday dear Jesus, Happy birthday this morn.
I'd like to sing about the gift
You gave the morning you were born.
Wake up you silent tombs. His life can play Love's tune
And find its way to listening ears.
His love can free you, dry your tears.
Oh, please receive this gift on Christmas morn.
He'd like to love you on this Christmas morn.

Happy birthday dear Jesus, Happy birthday this morn.

Oh Reader, if you don't have Jesus in your life, you are missing out on an amazing ride! I'm sorry for all of the hypocrisy Christians display today. But don't look at them, look at Him. I will fail you, but He never will.

Chapter Five: High School and Idols

*A*s I started getting to know the Lord better, He began to show me areas in my life that needed to be changed. He loved me just the same, but He saw unhealthy loves I depended on; loves I placed before Him. These are called idols. The Lord wants first place in our lives, not second or third. Ezekiel says: *"Men have set up idols in their hearts and have put them right before their faces. Should I let them inquire of Me at all?" (Ezekiel 14:3)*

Remember the lifelines I clung to before I met the Lord? Music and men (M & M) fought for first place in my heart, but God wanted that spot. I was never Daddy's little girl, so a huge gap remained in my soul that longed for a man's love, and, sadly, I allowed this longing to come before God.

Once I finished my year at P.C., I happily scampered off to M & M world. I can see now God's wisdom in placing me at P.C. for the first year of my new Christian walk because I grew without any distractions. But now that I was in M & M world, do you think Satan was just going to sit back and leave me alone? No. He knew very well what my weaknesses were, and he went right for the jugular.

Two significant things happened to me in high school. First, I met my high school sweetheart, Daryl. He was wonderful. My family loved him and I loved him. Everyone thought I would marry Daryl someday because, as young as we were, Daryl and I were a great fit. He was a serious musician so he and I spent hours playing guitar and singing together. But there was a catch: Daryl was not a Christian. At Monday Night Bible Study, I was just learning God's thoughts on being unequally yoked. I began to reconsider marrying Daryl.

I tried everything I could think of to get that boy interested in the Lord, but nothing worked. Diane kept reminding me that missionary dating is a risky business. That was the first M (men) in my struggle with M & M. I'll come back to Daryl in a minute.

While the first M was hard to let go of, the second M (music) was so important to me that the Lord had to step in and literally wrench it out of my grasp. Mo, Adrienne, (my younger sister), and I formed a musical trio that led to making some pretty decent money singing for weddings. All three of us played guitar by now, and we could harmonize on the spot. We sounded so much alike that no one could tell the difference between our voices. To this day when we listen to our old demos we get into arguments over who's singing what part.

Daryl

My sisters and I were harmonious when we were singing together, but in relating with each other... definitely *not*. We actually fought like cats and dogs, but the money was so good that we kept performing together anyway. We were hired for nicer and nicer weddings and eventually found ourselves singing at Liberace's home. I remember that the swimming pool of this world famous pianist and entertainer was shaped like a piano!

What an exciting day that was! I was sixteen, Mo was fourteen, and A was twelve. After the wedding, a producer from Capitol Records came up to us and said, "I want to record you girls...at Capitol Records." So off we went, just the three of us, into the heart of Hollywood. After recording about six wedding songs, the producer said, "I think you girls have what it takes to make it." Then, the real shocker: "My backers will pay for all expenses to promote you." You talk about a *Giant M*!

My sisters and I could hardly wait to get home and tell my parents. My mom listened quietly, and then said, "No." Just "No." She gave no reason, accepted no arguments. Just "No." We couldn't believe our ears.

> *"No." Just "No." She gave no reason, accepted no arguments. Just "No." We couldn't believe our ears.*

I have to tell you, all three of us were mad at my mom for years over that curt, unfeeling answer. But the Lord urged me to forgive her and gave me two words: "Let Go." Looking back now, I know God's grace and mercy were protecting me. I can't even imagine what my life would have been like had I followed that path. I've seen fame wreak havoc on a normal life. God wisely closed the door on that *Giant M*, and I'm extremely grateful that He did.

Now back to Daryl. After many hours of agonizing prayer and seeking wise, godly counsel, I finally broke up with him. We had been dating for three years and it took me a long time to muster up the courage. When I finally broke it off, Daryl's mom told me that he sat in a chair for two days...didn't eat...didn't drink...just sat and stared. I was miserable, too.

One night shortly after the breakup, Daryl showed up in my room at 2:00 a.m. in the morning. He climbed through my window and wasn't even quiet about it. There I was standing in the middle of my room while Daryl was on the floor holding on to my feet crying, begging me not to break up with him. I almost caved when my dad came bursting through the bedroom door. Of course I thought Dad was going to punch Daryl in the nose for being in my bedroom at this hour of the night, but instead my dad stopped short when he saw the tears running down Daryl's face and mine. In one of my father's shining moments, he gently lifted Daryl up and brought him outside where they talked for a good hour. I didn't know until then that my dad had a soft spot in matters of love.

Letting go of Daryl was one of the hardest things I've ever had to do. Losing Daryl left a gigantic void in my heart, but the

Lord filled it up...way up...with new friends, with Himself, and with a life so much better than the one I thought I wanted.

Next on the CD is a song the Lord used to give me the strength I needed to finally let go of Daryl. What do you think it's called? Take a guess.

Track#4: LET GO

Verse 1
I stood on the edge of a cliff looking down
A thousand feet to the ground.
He said, "Don't be afraid just step out in faith.
No, you won't go hurdling down."

> Chorus
> *"Let go, please let go. How will you ever know?*
> *That I'll catch you in my loving arms.*
> *I'm waiting so please let go."*

Verse 2
So I started to lean giving up all my dreams
And the desires that come before Him.
But I saw that 'ole tree reaching out to me saying,
"Fool, take hold of my limbs!"

> Chorus
> *"Let go, please let go. How will you ever know?*
> *That I'll catch you in my loving arms.*
> *I'm waiting so please let go.*
> *Let go.*
> *Let go.*
> *Let go!"*

Bridge
But I panicked, I can't do it Lord! I can see the tree its security.
But I can't see your hand Lord don't you understand? Faith is too hard for me.

Chorus
"Let go, please let go. How will you ever know?
That I'll catch you in my loving arms.
I'm waiting so please let go.
Let go.
Let go.
Let go!"

Verse 3
Then I started to fall and I made Him my all
Letting Him do the work in my heart.
Then I was set free and then I could see.
He gave me what I desired from the start.
Now all the pressure is gone as I rest in his arms,
And I know that my fears were in vain.
If those fears are in you, please believe it's true.
I bet He's waiting to do the same for you.

Chorus
Let go, please let go. How will you ever know?
That He'll catch you in His loving arms.
He's waiting, so please let go.
Let go.
Let go.
Let go.
Let go!

At this point in my PJs Conferences, I ask the attending women to write down a list of idols they are holding on to. Then, the women and I symbolically give them up. It's serious business. Afterwards, I treat them to a little fun with an audience participation song that lightens the mood, but still makes a point. Remember the old song, "Fifty Ways to Leave Your Lover?" Well, this song is called "Ten Ways to lose an Idol." It's number Five on the CD.

Track#5: TEN WAYS TO LOSE AN IDOL

1. Ya gotta take that idol and drop it on the floor.(3x)
What are you clinging to that old thing for?
Take that idol and drop it on the floor.

> *2. Ya gotta take that idol and put it on the shelf. (3x)*
> *'Cause Christ demands allegiance to nothin' but Himself.*
> *Take that idol and put it on the shelf.*

3. Ya gotta take that idol and kick it out the door. (3x)
You and I both know you don't need it anymore.
Take that idol and kick it out the door.

> *4. Ya gotta take that idol and throw it far away. (3x)*
> *I know it's hard, but ya gotta obey.*
> *Take that idol and throw it far away.*

5. Ya gotta take that idol and toss it in the air. (3x)
Don't ya think you serve Him better with it out of your hair?
Take that idol and toss it in the air.

> *6. Ya gotta take that idol and go and press delete. (3x)*
> *'Cause livin' for the Lord you are completely complete.*
> *Take that idol and go and press delete.*

7. Ya gotta take that idol and put it on a bus. (3x)
Now wave goodbye and don't you make no fuss.
Take that idol and put it on a bus.

> *8. Ya gotta take that idol and ship it out to sea. (3x)*
> *You'll see more clearly and you'll be set free.*
> *Take that idol and ship it out to sea.*

9. Ya gotta take that idol and throw it overboard. (3x)
Then sail that boat with just you and the Lord.
Take that idol and throw it overboard.

10. Ya gotta take those idols and give 'em to the Lord. (3x)
This song is finally over here's my very last chord!

Chapter Six: College and Cavalcade

After the big breakup, my mom sat me down and suggested that I date a lot of different guys like she did. That sounded good to me so, upon entering college, I went on the prowl. I landed what I thought was a dream job at a men's clothing shop where I just kept meeting one really nice Christian guy after another. It's amazing the conversations you can have while measuring a man's inseams.

Honestly, I am a little embarrassed to say this, but, at one point, I was dating twenty-three guys at one time. I'm not lying! My mom had to keep a calendar of my dates so that she could

My favorite class in college was the cafeteria.

keep track and not call the wrong guy by the wrong name. On any given Saturday, I might have breakfast and tennis with one guy, lunch and the beach with the next guy, and then dinner and a movie with another. I would make sure my date dropped me off in back of the house while the other date sat waiting in the front living room with the outside window curtains closed. My mom and I had this routine down to a science! I remember one time I was in such a hurry between dates that I accidentally dropped my curling iron in the toilet. Only half my hair was curled so I jumped in my car and sped to a friend's house to borrow her curling iron. The guy waiting never even knew I left and came back! I loved those living room curtains!

What my mom assumed I understood was that, when she was dating, she told each of her "fellas" about the other "fellas" she was dating. Somehow I missed that part. So, when Christmas rolled around, all my men thought they were coming over for Christmas dinner. This is my mom's shining moment. (I think she felt a little responsible for her advice.) She helped me bake twenty-three plates of cookies, decorate them like Christmas trees, write apology notes for each, and then load them all into our station wagon. Then, bless her heart, she drove with me to every house to deliver them. I spent Christmas alone with no boyfriend that year, but I learned my lesson and quit the men's shop.

Except for the dating part, I hated college. I was such a flibbertigibbet and had no discipline at all. I made terrible grades (except for the music courses) plus I constantly missed classes due to my marathon dating. I even disliked the music courses because they were too easy and boring. The professors kept sending me out of the room to help struggling students. I thought, "I'm paying good money for these courses. They should be paying *me* if I'm going to be used as a teacher." Unfortunately, I made a really foolish decision, but it seemed right at the time: I quit school. This decision meant I had to move out of my parents' home because, at eighteen years of age, I had to be "out of the house" if I wasn't in school full time.

I was really excited to get out from under my parents' roof because, for one reason, I wanted to pick out my own church.

I was really excited to get out from under my parents' roof anyway because, for one reason, I wanted to pick out my own church. I had made a deal with my dad, that as long as I was going to the Monday Night Bible Study, I would also attend the Catholic Church on Sundays. Well, once I was out from under his roof, all bets were off baby! Right as I was planning my "breakout," the Lord sent me the most wonderful gift: my cousin Vicky (no, not Vinny) from New York.

I had never met Vicky face to face but we were committed

Kathy and Vicky

pen pals. She was looking to break out too, so we felt like two peas in a pod. Vicky and I both got waitress jobs and started our new independent lives. I remember the tiny little apartment we shared had only one bedroom and two twin beds. On our first Sunday at the apartment, we jumped up and down on our beds like little kids singing, "We get to go to any church we want to! Na na na na na!" Oh, the taste of freedom! She and I visited several churches but finally decided on a little house church that Diane and Roger attended called Diamond Bar Christian Fellowship.

Dr. Jack Welch was the pastor and a no-nonsense, ex-naval officer. Jack was, and still is, one of the godliest men I have ever met. As you will see later, Jack's family, including his wife, Pat, and daughter, Sheryl, a licensed therapist, became an important part of my life. They impacted my entire family for years to come, and, by marriage, are now a part of my extended family.

Pastor Jack Welch and his wife, Pat

One Sunday night, Vicky and I went to a Christian concert to hear a group called "Cavalcade." They were on tour 365 days a year and hit all fifty states. One of their female singers had to fly home because her mom was gravely ill. At the concert, the director announced that Cavalcade was looking for a female vocalist to take her place immediately. They also announced that auditions were being held after the concert. Vicky kept poking me with her elbow saying, "Try out! This is perfect for you!"

Well, two weeks later I was on the road. I'm thankful that Vicky was such a trouper with me leaving so abruptly. Fortunately for her, all three of her sisters moved to L.A. shortly after I left.

Within the first month of being on the road, I came to the stark realization that my days of being a flibbertigibbet were over. Cavalcade was a serious ministry and they expected 100 percent effort from every member of the team. "Discipline" was a big word around there.

One of Cavalcade's expectations really annoyed me. Every morning, no matter how early we had to leave for the next concert, we were required to go off and find a quiet place to have a "Quiet Time" with the Lord. I thought this was a huge infringement on my

Cavalcade Singers

sleep and I complained about it profusely...until someone informed me that complaining wasn't allowed on this tour...ever. "So," I thought, "I could always sleep. They'll never know. I'll just say I was praying with my eyes closed."

This fine plan worked for a while, but after a few weeks someone got wise to it. As we pulled out of the parking lot each morning, the director started asking us to share what the Lord had showed us during our time with Him. "Yikes!" I thought, "I'd better get cracking." Then, if that wasn't bad enough, the director also gave us one Bible verse a week to memorize.

"What gall!" I thought.

But here's what happened: The other members began to share what the Lord had shown them during their Quiet Times, preparing them with the exact scripture to make it through the day. I'd get chills hearing how the Lord would warn one of the members about an unforeseen situation before it happened. A few even likened themselves to soldiers at war. Each morning, God equipped them with a specific piece of armor for each day's battle. They would share how they had an agenda for the day but the Lord would completely change it, always for the better. These Christians were genuinely excited to meet Him every morning to get their "Marching Orders."

After a while, their excitement wore off on me. I started doing the "Quiet Time" thing and I want to tell you something: twenty-eight years and about 10,000 Quiet Times later, I still get butterflies in my stomach when the Lord speaks to me before my day starts. If I miss one, I really feel cheated, like I missed out on my marching orders for that day. The next song on the CD is called Marching Orders.

Track#6: MARCHING ORDERS

Chorus
Ya gotta get your marching orders from the Lord.
Then you'll never be too busy or too bored.
Don't try to start your day any other way.
Ya gotta get your marching orders from the Lord.

Verse 1
Jehoshaphat saw his enemies coming,
Far too many to fight.
His heart was pounding and his knees were weak.
He was completely overcome with fright.
But he got down on his knees
And he said to the Lord, "Oh please!"
"Show us what to do. We trust in you!"

Well, the battle was won right there
And prayer was the key.

Chorus
Ya gotta get your marching orders from the Lord.
Then you'll never be too busy or too bored.
Don't try to start your day any other way.
Ya gotta get your marching orders from the Lord.

Verse 2
Joshua saw his enemies coming.
They looked pretty easy to fight.
His heart was proud and his memory was weak.
He said, "Piece of cake, this must be right!"
But he forgot to get on his knees.
He suffered 36 casualties.
Joshua learned that day that it pays to pray
'Cause the battles that look so easy,
Well … they may not be!

Chorus
Ya gotta get your marching orders from the Lord.
Then you'll never be too busy or too bored.
Don't try to start your day any other way.
Ya gotta get your marching orders from the Lord.

Bridge
Satan's armies may come against us.
Our first response is to try and flee.
But the Lord Jehovah is always with us.
He is willing to fight the battle for you and for me.

Ending Chorus:
Ya gotta get your marching orders from the Lord.
Then you'll never be too busy or too bored.

Don't try to start your day any other way.
Ya gotta get your marching orders from the Lord.

Don't try to start your day ... your own way.
Ya gotta get your marching orders from the Lord.

Don't try to start your day without your battle array.
Ya gotta get your marching orders from the Lord.

Don't try to start your day, get on your knees and pray!
Ya gotta get your marching orders from the Lord.

The Blessed Years

Chapter Seven: Elaine

*W*hile touring the country with Cavalcade, I really missed my mom. As much as I loved my independence, a whole year had passed since I'd seen her, and I just missed her sometimes. One night we performed at a church in little old Jackson, Michigan. After the concert, I slipped away for some time alone. I found a kindergarten Sunday school room with little baby chairs in it, one of which sat in the middle of a big round "story time" carpet. I sat down in the little chair and put my face in my hands praying, "Lord, I wish I could see my mommy right now!" A couple of tears slipped down my cheeks when, all of a sudden, the door burst open and in bounced this energetic woman who, strangely enough, looked just like my mom.

Elaine and Kathy

I blinked a couple of times before almost falling off the chair. She smiled and said, "Hello Honey, my name is Mrs. Blackmore, but you can call me Mrs. B. Get your coat on sweetie, you are staying at my house tonight." I cheered up immediately, eager to soak up all the mothering I could from Mrs. B. When we arrived at her house I met her four daughters, one of whom was named Elaine. Elaine was not thrilled to meet me. I found out later it was because she had driven down from college specifically to soak up some lovin' from her mom that night. Elaine did not want to share and I certainly could not blame her!

Mrs. B. said, "Come on everyone, we are taking Kathy out for ice cream." I couldn't wait to sit next to Mrs. B. and chat away. Before we were seated at the restaurant, I snuck off to the powder

Kathy and Elaine unedited

room. I assumed Mrs. B. would save a seat for me right next to her; after all, I was the guest of honor. But when I came back from the ladies' room, to my utter dismay, I discovered that Mrs. B. was nestled into a booth with her husband and three daughters, and no room for me! I stood there confused for a minute until Mrs. B. smiled and pointed to a small table for two, all the way on the other side of the restaurant.

There, at that tiny table, was Elaine sitting across from the empty seat with her arms folded, looking madder than a hornet. I made my way over to her table and slumped down into the chair, disappointment written all over my face. We just glared at each other for a good five minutes. Well, you'll never guess. By the time the ice cream was gone, Elaine and I knew God had ordained our meeting. I don't know if two women can be soul mates, but we've been the closest thing to it for thirty-four years.

Track#7: THE BALLAD OF KATHY AND ELAINE

Verse 1
Sitting across from a strange unknown face,
A meeting forced in a faraway place.
Both lips are set to be very polite.
Both minds expecting the talk to be light.
Whoever thought that my heart would unite
With this person who messed up my plans for the night?

> Chorus
> *One heart, one mind,*
> *One love, the kindred kind.*
> *A better friend who could find?*
> *Than Elaine, the one whose heart's*
> *Like mine ... like mine.*

Verse 2
We walked and we talked in the cool midnight air
Later and later but we didn't care.
Tucked in our beds we found more dreams to share
Deeper and deeper as deep as we dared.
The sun it came up without one wink of sleep...The
Dawn of new friendship in Christ it would keep.

> Chorus
> *One heart, one mind,*
> *One love, the kindred kind.*
> *A better friend who could find?*
> *Than Elaine, the one whose heart's*
> *Like mine ... like mine...like mine...like mine...like mine.*

Verse 3
We went separate ways vows were made, "Keep in touch!"
Her letters consistent, but mine not so much.
Our friendship continued a few years and then
The grace of God brought us together again.
What joy on that morning to look at her smile.
I thought she'd be sticking around for a while.

> Bridge
> *Friendships like these come once in a lifetime.*
> *Cherish them, cultivate, pray and protect them.*
> *In the darkest of times they may be your life line*
> *To love you back to the Father again.*

Verse 4
Now comes the hard part the part I can't sing
Without blinking my eyes as the tears start to sting.
I miss you Elaine and I wish you were here.
The day that you left it brought heartache and fear.
But God's called you little Abraham to a land far away.
What comfort to know in His will you will stay.

> Bridge
> *Friendships like these come once in a lifetime.*
> *Cherish them, cultivate, pray.*
> *In the darkest of times they may be your life line*
> *To love you back to the Father again.*

Chorus
One heart, one mind,
One love, the kindred kind.
A better friend who could find?
Than Elaine, the one whose heart's like mine.

Chapter Eight:
Home Again Home Again Jiggity Jig

Spiritually, I grew by leaps and bounds while I was on the road, but physically I shrunk. I lost over forty pounds due to the grueling schedule. Being on tour was exhausting work, but I loved it. As much as I enjoyed singing about the Lord 365 days a year, when I hit eighty pounds I knew it was time to leave. Mom said I could come back home until I found a job and a place to live. Vicky's apartment was filled up with her three sisters by then.

When I walked off the plane in Los Angeles, I passed by a big banner that said, "Welcome Home!" My family was hiding behind that sign, but never jumped out to welcome me because they didn't recognize me. I walked right on by and went to the baggage claim to look for them. I was so thin my own family didn't even know who I was.

When I got to the house, I remember sleeping for days and days before I joined the real world again. Just as I was starting to recover, my dad announced that I needed to move out. He gave me a deadline of one month to find a job and an apartment. He also showed me a financial graph that he had drawn a few years earlier. In other words, he let me know, in no uncertain terms, that my living there did not coincide with his graph.

Because both my parents had supported their moms, my dad expected his kids to be very independent when it came to money. But the blunt way he presented it, using a graph and financial statistics, stung a little. On top of this, I felt I needed more time to recover. Before you judge my father too harshly, I should tell you one quirky thing about him: he is "Mr. Precise."

He worked on the Apollo space crafts, where extreme accuracy was essential. If my dad said, "I will pick you up at 7:04," then, sure enough, you'd better be ready at exactly 7:04. I read the graph and hit the pavement.

When the deadline arrived, I still hadn't been hired anywhere but Dad wouldn't budge, believing I hadn't tried hard enough. My spiritual parents, Diane and Roger, came to the rescue. They made room for me in their little house, along with their two young children. I slept in the living room on a pull-out couch which I'm sure didn't fit into their financial plan. But they trusted the Lord to meet their needs and took me in, no strings attached and no rent required. They made me feel like I was a part of their family and that meant the world to me. Just five days after I moved in, a bank around the corner hired me.

Bedtime routine with Toby and Sarah

God was sovereign and, as angry as I was at my dad, I can see why the Lord wanted me to live with Diane and Roger. Theirs was a godly marriage and I was privileged to see firsthand how to train up children in the ways of the Lord. I had no clue that other parents tucked their kids in at night, told them bedtime stories, read the Bible to them, and prayed together. This bedtime routine was totally foreign to me, and I enjoyed being a part of it.

What I really wanted to do was go back to school. I was a little nervous about my grades, but hoped that Cavalcade had drilled some discipline into me. I also believed that if the Lord was telling me to go back to school, then He could provide whatever I needed to be successful, as long as I let Him guide me.

And guide me He did! Wait until you hear this! My pastor, Dr. Jack, offered a three-year discipleship class at church. Now remember, Jack was a naval officer, so his middle name was discipline. Did you know that the word discipline and disciple come from the same root word? That three-year discipleship course changed my life.

I remember the first day sitting in the discipleship class at Jack's house with about twenty other people there. I looked around and realized there were a lot of smart cookies in that room and I wasn't one of them. Jack read the syllabus to us and I started thinking, "This is way too hard. I can't pull this off."

He wanted us to read four spiritual books a month and write book reports on each of them. He also asked us to hand in weekly schedules of what we did every fifteen minutes to show us how much time we waste. Jack wanted to teach us skills in time management, goal setting, and prioritizing our days according to scriptural principles. Another important part of the class was to train us how to study the Bible with the tools like those used by seminary students.

When Jack announced, "Discipline means to train by pain," I started sinking lower and lower into my chair.

"I don't *like* pain," I whined to myself as his voice became one big blur. I left that night never intending to return to the class. After all, I rationalized, I was working full time and the class *was* on Wednesday night—spaghetti night.

I left that night never intending to return to the class. After all, I rationalized, I was working full time and the class was on Wednesday night—spaghetti night.

Okay, you are not going to believe this: the next Wednesday night as I was slurping up a delicious strand of spaghetti, the Lord said my name. It scared me to death and I looked around to see if anybody else had heard it. Then He said, "Kathy! Put...the fork...down...and go to class."

I was so stunned that I simply spit the spaghetti out of my mouth, mumbled "Gotta go," and headed out the door. My family all stared at me in disbelief. If you had known me then, you would definitely know that my leaving a full plate of spaghetti on the table was pretty amazing in itself. I drove straight to Jack's. When I got there, the lights were out and I thought maybe they had canceled class. But again, the Lord nudged me forward: "Go!"

"Okay, Okay!" I said.

I went around back and noticed the class was watching a movie called "Outward Bound," a program that takes willing participants to a deserted island and helps them overcome incredible hurdles. (This was way before "Survivor.") The participants would jump in ice cold water or scale cliffs. I heard testimony after testimony of regular Joes saying: "I never thought I could do this;" or, "I found out when I pushed my body it would do things I never thought possible," or, "I realized I can do anything I set my mind to."

"When I get home," one participant said, "I'm going to make some major changes."

Then the movie went on to show that the participants did indeed achieve amazing accomplishments once they got home. It was very inspiring! I think Jack showed that movie to encourage us. And boy, it did. The Lord spoke to me one more time that night: He said, "You can do this. We can do this." And we did.

Living with Diane and Roger was the perfect setting for me to complete that discipleship course. I had no other responsibilities outside of work, except to fold up my couch in the mornings and show up for dinner at night. In order to complete a book a week, I read during my lunch hour every day. I would bring a lawn chair to work, sit outside the library across from the bank in the warm California sun, and study. Remember those smart cookies from the class? Well, most of them dropped out. God and I stuck with it for the entire three years and there were only two students in the class who completed all of the assignments by graduation day: Julie Anderson, a good friend from Diane's Bible study, and...guess who? Me, the flibbertigibbet...and my awesome Father.

Now, with the skills I'd learned, I was ready for college. When I went back, instead of squeaking by with poor grades, I got straight A's. Flibbertigibbet…A's. My brain hadn't changed or morphed since the last time I tried college, but my discipline, time management skills, and relationship with the Lord had. I was getting my marching orders from Him every morning now.

I even remember breaking up with a guy because he kept calling me during my morning study hours to chat.

"The nerve of that guy!" I thought. I had made it very clear to him that he could call me any time after noon but he just didn't get it. Can you imagine me being this disciplined during my first round of college? Not a chance.

With this second round of college came some other changes too. I left the bank and started working at a Music Conservatory. I said goodbye to Diane and Roger, spread my wings, and moved into a big house with four godly women. My roommates included Vicky and Elaine, who had just moved out from Michigan. We had a blast living together.

By then, Vicky was a math teacher and she would tutor me every afternoon as we tanned in the back yard—another of God's provisions! Vicky was a wonderful teacher! I remember after I aced a geometry final, the math professor drove to my house, knocked on the door and accused me of cheating. Apparently no one had ever aced his geometry final before. I clearly remember Vicky saying, in her New York accent, "He's got a lot of nerve coming to our house. We could call the police for harassment." She was a spit-fire!

What fun times we had! The gals called me "Crash Car Kathy." Thinking back on it, I guess I was a little accident prone. (That hasn't changed much.) Our house had a central vacuum system and one morning I decided to vacuum my car with it. So I pulled the vacuum hose out through the front door and parked my car on the lawn facing the front picture window. You know where this is going don't you?

The hose wasn't quite long enough so I got in my car to inch it closer to the house. All of a sudden, the next thing I knew, I was sitting on the grass looking at my car which had smashed into the front window. Everyone in the house came running out thinking there had been an earthquake. They kept looking at me and the car and then me and the house which, by the way, had a huge crack in it from top to bottom. I was scratching my head because I couldn't remember how it happened.

Well, apparently, I panicked when a bee flew into my car and I jumped out of the car which popped the clutch and caused the car to lurch forward, hitting the house. That was the year I also fell off a ski lift. Believe me, you don't want to know.

Those years were some of the best of my life so I often refer to them as the blessed years. Oh, I almost forgot, I met an entrepreneur at the music conservatory and together we opened up our own school of voice and piano. By the time I was twenty-six, I had my name up on a huge sign in the middle of downtown and I was on top of the world. God was blessing me with:

A great living situation

A great career

A great reputation

A great year at school

Everything was great, great, great!

And then…Crash!

And I'm not talking about a picture window. One foolish decision changed everything and caused me to enter into the most painful fifteen years of my life.

Luke 6:46 says: *"Why do you call me, 'Lord, Lord,' and do not do what I say? I will show you what he is like who comes to me and hears my words and puts them into practice. He is like a man building a house, who dug down deep and laid the foundation on rock. When a flood came, the torrent struck that house but could not shake it, because it was well built. But the one who hears my words and does not put them into practice is like a man who built a house on the ground without a foundation. The moment the torrent struck that house, it collapsed and its destruction was complete."*

That was me. I closed my ears and made a major life-changing decision without Him.

The Painful Years

Chapter Nine: Kathy Gets Married

I srael's history in the Old Testament bears a striking resemblance to my life at this point. Remember how the Israelites kept asking God for a king? God wanted to be their one and only king, but no, they wanted a person they could physically see and touch. God answered Israel's request, and granted them human kings, but eventually the nation of Israel was led into sin by these earthly kings. Furthermore, God allowed outside nations to come in and conquer Israel, making them slaves.

Well, I wanted a king: a husband.

I thought I was an old maid at twenty-seven. I remember sitting in the college library one fateful day. (If I could go back in time and live that day over again, I certainly would.) Staring down at my boring textbook, I was thinking, "I totally do not get this assignment. I'm so sick of school right now."

Then, my gaze lazily wandered out the window into the beautiful spring day, and I said to myself, "I'm tired and I deserve a break." I reached into my sweater pocket for a piece of gum and found a wad of paper with a phone number scribbled on it. I remembered the phone number was given to me by a really cute guy from church. Now, this was during my morning study time. Remember my rule?

As I looked down at that number, I heard the Holy Spirit's still, small voice say, "Don't do it, Kathy. Take a break, but then go right back to studying."

"But Lord, this guy is so cute. He looks just like Donny Osmond and I am really sick of studying today!"

As I stood up to go call him, I heard the voice again saying to me, *"No!"* just as clear as a bell. But did I listen? No. This was a weak area for me and I wanted a king. Have you ever come to a fork in the road where one decision would alter the course of your entire life? Have you ever looked back and wondered what your life would be like had you chosen differently?

My first wedding

This was my fork in the road and I chose to ignore my Father's voice.

Hebrews 3:8 says, *"Today if you hear His voice, do not harden your heart as when they provoked me in the wilderness."*

Verse 3:11 says, *"I swore in my wrath that they shall not enter my rest."*

Verse 3:18 says, *"And to whom did He swear that they would not enter His rest, but to those who were disobedient. So we see that they were not able to enter because of unbelief."*

Sin is unbelief. It's disbelieving that God knows what He's doing. That small act of disobedience led me down a path that caused me unrest for years. I am a sinner and the Lord has forgiven me, but the pain I caused myself, and eventually others, was irreversible. Was God surprised? Was He caught off guard? No. He saw ahead and I can just imagine Him shaking His head saying, "You are heading down the wrong road, Kathy. This is not my best for you."

> *He saw ahead and I can just imagine Him shaking His head saying, "You are heading down the wrong road, Kathy. This is not my best for you."*

Now back to the story. Here's what happened. I went to "Donny's" and fell head over heels in love with...his roommate! Steve was a tall, blond Italian who was extremely intelligent and athletic. Since I don't have Steve's permission to relate to you the details about our marriage, I am going to try and stick to what God did for me in a bad situation.

Let's start here. Those close to Steve and I saw glaring red flags in the relationship. Pastor Jack, Diane and Roger, and my family brought many of these red flags to our attention, but Steve and I assured them we were "in love" so all would be wonderful. Even at our rehearsal dinner, my mom pulled me aside and said, "Kathleen, this doesn't feel right. Are you sure you want to do this?"

I'm sorry, but I must get on my soap box here for a minute. If you are happily married to the love of your life, you can skip this part.

Ladies, if you are looking for Mr. Right, or maybe you think you have found him—*please, please*—I am begging you (I'm actually on my knees right now) seek wise counsel from those you trust. Go to those who know you and love you and get some feedback. Most good parents or parental figures love their children and don't want to see their children suffer pain. Take advantage of their wisdom and bring what they say to the Lord in earnest prayer. No matter how much you and Mr. Wonderful have in common, if you two are unequally yoked, you are going to have a rough go of it.

Like Diane said, "Missionary dating is a very risky business." By unequally yoked, I'm not just talking about a Christian marrying a non-Christian; I'm also talking about marrying a man who isn't the spiritual leader in the relationship. If your man isn't a spiritual leader, then wait for one. Whether you wait for signs that your man is growing into a spiritual leader, or you wait for someone else who already is a spiritual leader, the operative word here is "wait."

Why do I say this so emphatically? One word...pain. I'm talking about pain like you've never felt before. I often hear the following words from young women in love, "But, he might come around. I'm praying for him."

If the Lord has specifically said to you, "Marry this man," and you see him growing by leaps and bounds, and you see a soft heart towards God, then that's different. But more often than not, when I ask a starry-eyed wannabe bride if the Lord has called her to this man, I get silence and averted eyes.

Let me ask you a question, girls. If the "God of this Universe," the creator of all things, could make a non-spiritual man with all these incredible qualities that you just can't live without, don't you think the "God of this Universe" could make a Christian version of that? And...if the "God of this Universe" did fashion such a man, don't you think that the "God of this Universe" could bring him your way? Do you think the "God of this Universe" is big enough for that task? He is, after all, (say it with me) the "God of this Universe" and He loves you and knows what you need better than you even know yourself.

I believe in parental matchmaking. I do; the parent being: (one more time) the "God of this Universe."

I married that tall, blond Italian and plugged my ears to all warnings because I wanted a king. At first Steve and I had some good times. We were in love. But because I had such a huge void in my heart that longed for a man's approval, I started making choices to please Steve no matter what it did to me. I dropped out of school and never went back. Every dime I made at the conservatory went towards his schooling.

On our wedding day, we got into a terrible fight. Amazingly, we stopped speaking to each other at our own wedding. The morning after the wedding, I woke up with a huge pit in my stomach and thought, "What have I done?"

I married so that I wouldn't grow old alone, but quickly found out that my family had been right all along. I was already totally alone. Listen to me. There's nothing more painful than being alone in a marriage. Thankfully, God is sovereign and He used this pain to draw me back to Him. All was forgiven, but I had a rough road ahead.

Not listening to my Father's voice that day at the library set me on a path of pain and heartache, as this next skit illustrates.

Track# 8: FORGIVE AND FORGET

There once was a girl who made a bad choice.
She chose to ignore her own Father's voice.
He told her, as they sat in His warm, cozy home,
"If you walk down that road, you walk it alone."

The moment her foot stepped away from the door,
The house grew dim, not bright like before.
She shivered because her heart had turned cold.
And she couldn't remember the truths she'd been told.

All she could think of was what lie ahead.
All she could hear were the words of the dead.
"Your Father's a liar, He couldn't love you,
Not half as much as you know I do."

"I am your comfort," sin said with a smile,
"So why not enjoy yourself, stay for a while."

And so she stayed long into the night.
How could something so comforting not be alright?

When she woke up it was like a bad dream.
Things were not good or as nice as they'd seemed.
She was a prisoner and the price of her sin?
She was more alone than she'd ever been.

"Sin has deceived me!" she said to the night.
"I want to be back in my own Father's light
To sit and chat by the warmth of the fire."
She burst through the gates shouting, "You are the Liar!"

She never looked back as she ran to His door,
Loving her Father even more than before.
But all of sudden she stopped dead in her tracks.
If He knew what she'd done He would not take her back.

So she sat on the porch where her sin had begun.
"He couldn't possibly forgive me for what I have done."
Her face in her hands, she cried and she cried.
Then she heard a faint voice saying, "Child, come inside."

The door swung wide open as he beckoned her in.
"I know what you did." He said. "I saw your sin."
She couldn't look him straight in the face, So ashamed
That He'd seen her in that awful place.

"Sit down by the fire and let's have a chat."
It felt good to sit where she'd always sat.
"The fact that you're here and not there let's me know
That you're serious about letting that other place go."

He lifted her chin, looked her straight in the eye.
"I forgive you," He said but he started to cry.
"I'm crying because I know what sin can do.
It will cause you some pain and some others pain too."

He reached into his pocket then held out his fist.
He reached for her hand to give her a gift.
As a tiny brown cross dropped into her palm,
She was overcome with an unexplainable calm.

She could look at her Father without guilt or fear,
As He whispered, "For those who have ears to hear,
It may seem impossible, hopeless and yet,
Because of this cross, I forgive and forget."

During my conferences, this is the point in the story when I have to ask the soundmen to leave. It's much harder to explain in person what happened next than it is to write about it in the privacy of my own home. I want to talk about my honeymoon. Don't worry, it's not "R" rated. I just have something to tell you that is meant for women only. I'm assuming you know about the birds and the bees. If you don't, then close the book and go ask Mom if she's ready to tell you.

About three days into our honeymoon, I called my mom from Jamaica and said, "Mom, how long before you liked...you know...the *deed*?"

She said, "Kathleen, I have eight kids. What do you think?"

I said, "I know Mom, but how long until you liked it?" I could almost hear her blush over the phone.

"I liked it right away. Why?"

"Well," I said, "for me it was the most excruciatingly painful thing I have ever experienced. On a pain scale from one to ten, it was about a twelve."

"That doesn't sound right," she said. "You'd better see a doctor when you get back."

When I got back from what felt like the longest two weeks of my life, I called my gynecologist right away. He sent me to a specialist and, after extensive testing, I found out that I had a rare degenerative disease called "lichen sclerosus et atrophicus dystrophy."

This disease was genetic, passed down from someone in my family line.

This is how I understood what was explained to me. I'm not a doctor, so bear with me. Somehow, my body has non-working progesterone. Progesterone has little receptors that receive the hormone testosterone and assimilates it into the skin throughout a woman's body making her...well...a woman. My cells' inability to accept testosterone caused deterioration of the skin from the inside out exposing raw nerves. That's why the "deed' was so painful.

At that time there was no cure. I was given two options. One option was that I could go through what the doctors called "male hormone therapy." I remember the specialist saying, "Well, your voice will lower, you will grow hair on your face, and you will basically start to look and feel like a man. You could just go the whole way and change over."

Can you imagine? He was telling me that I would be going from a soprano to a bass in the course of a few years!

The other option was not much better—surgery to remove everything and I would basically become like a eunuch, with no ability to have sexual sensation at all. The doctor said to think about it and make a decision soon because more skin was deteriorating by the day.

I remember driving back from UCLA and thinking, "How am I going to tell Steve?"

"Hello honey, I'm home and oh, by the way, I may have to become a man. What do you think?"

At this point, neither of us had the emotional health nor the communication skills to handle this correctly. We fought. I prayed. Every day I entreated the Lord, asking Him, "Lord, which should I choose?"

I really didn't want to become a man. I sadly resolved that surgery was the only alternative, but every time I prayed about it, the Lord said, "Wait." That is exactly what I told my specialist every time he called me for a decision. He was an old Jewish guy who looked like Santa, twinkle in his eyes and all. He was great. I told him that I was a Christian and that I knew my Lord's voice, and "wait" meant wait. The doctor said, "Well, you can't wait long."

After nine months of hearing "wait" over and over again from the Lord, my doctor finally called and said, "Look Kathy, your skin is deteriorating by the day. I am going to have to drop you as a noncompliant patient if you don't make a decision today."

He told me that I had to come out there that day and give him an answer.

So I drove out to his office, praying the whole time, "Lord tell me what to say, tell me what to do." I was so distraught, my hands broke out in hives. When I arrived at the specialist's office, he was on the phone but motioned me in. He had tears in his eyes. He put the phone down and said, "You are not going to believe this. That was Johns Hopkins University calling me to say that this very morning their researchers discovered a way to replace the faulty progesterone and rebuild your damaged cells! They have been working on a compound for a long time and finally got it right. They expect great results and are predicting that you should be back to normal in about a year."

I remember I was leaning against the door and I just slid down to the floor and sobbed and sobbed in gratefulness to the Lord. I also sputtered out something like, "Maybe Steve will love me now." The old doctor put his arm around me and told me that my insurance company would pay for free counseling. That's when I met Sheryl.

Chapter Ten: The "C" Words

I mentioned before that Pastor Jack's daughter, Sheryl, was a therapist. I took the old doctor's advice and made an appointment to see her for counseling. Of course, I went in to my first session saying: my husband is this and that and everything else. After listening to my raving for several minutes, Sheryl quietly said, "Why don't we work on you first?"

That was *not* what I wanted to hear. Nevertheless, Sheryl gave me a test which revealed I was quite dysfunctional. "Co-dependent," she called it; I had never even heard that word before. I said, "You don't understand, I'm here to talk about...*him*." She said, "We'll get to him later."

For the next year, as we worked on me, I learned so much from Sheryl. I learned how to nurture myself by looking in the mirror every day and saying, "It's me and you and God. We're the only ones who are ultimately responsible for building up this low emotional bank account."

Sheryl

Sheryl explained to me that, "If your bank account has only two dollars in it, and someone takes out one or two dollars, then the results are devastating."

"But" she went on, "if your bank account has one hundred dollars in it, one dollar taken out doesn't hurt so much."

She told me that my emotional bank account was at a real low, and it was crucial that I build it back up. Did you know that it takes at least ten positive statements to offset one negative? So, the question was, how was I going to build up my bank account?

Sheryl asked me to write every positive trait I could think of about myself on one side of a sheet of paper, and, on the other side, write every negative trait. Well, I easily filled the negative side to the brim, even running out of paper—but the good side? I could think of only two positive traits about myself: I'm talented and pretty. That's it. A quick word to moms: you probably know this, but it is so important to daily reaffirm your daughters' inner qualities, those unique traits that you love about them. Keep building their bank accounts!

After reading my paper, Sheryl gave me an assignment: write a letter to all of my friends asking them to make a list of the inner qualities they loved about me, but...they couldn't mention talent or looks as those were external. She hoped I could draw from this list to start building my emotional bank account with the nurturing I never received as a child. My friends came through and I bawled like a baby when I read those letters. I still have them. A year later, after daily studying those letters, I could completely fill the good page and barely fill the bad.

As I changed, the way in which I related to Steve and others changed—I stopped being a doormat. I learned effective communication tools and shared them with him and my family. I hung a list of those tools on my refrigerator door so I could look at them whenever a family member called. As I grew stronger and more self-assured, my poor family did not know what to do with me. All of a sudden, their old tricks weren't working on me anymore. When my siblings saw these changes, some of them came to me with their own issues, so I sent them straight to Sheryl. You don't know how *huge* that was. Back then, my family did not view counseling as a helpful alternative. They were afraid of the whole process, and called it the "C" word. That's a funny, quirky thing my family does: if we don't like something, if it's *really* bad, we don't say the whole name. Thus, counseling was dubbed the "C" word.

These changes in me happened right around the same time God asked me to start praying for my sister, Mo. Pastor Jack used to say that the verse, "Go, and make disciples" should actually be translated "*As* you go, make disciples."

Jack would ask us, "You go somewhere every day, don't you?" Then he would say, "As you go, you don't just *do* a ministry, you *are* a ministry. Basically, you are missionaries wherever you go." Jack challenged us to ask the Lord, specifically, who we should pray for in our daily "somewheres" and then try to invest time in those individuals. I liked that idea. With my busy schedule, honing in on just a few individuals sounded do-able to me.

I remember sitting on my bed and asking the Lord who I should invest in. I sat waiting patiently for someone's name to pop into my mind. As clear as a bell, I heard:

"Mo."

"Uh…come again, Lord?"

"Mo!"

"Mo??? Nooooo!! Don't you remember, Lord? She's the one I held a kitchen knife over? Please Lord. No!!" I was being honest with Him. "I can't do it, Lord. Not her. Can you give me someone else; door number two?"

And this is what the Lord said to me, "Just start praying for her everyday and watch Me work. Does praying for Mo cause you to suffer in any way?"

"No"

"Are you bleeding when you pray?"

"Well…no."

"Are you hanging on a cross when you pray?"

"Again, no."

"Then just pray."

"Okay, Lord. I can do that."

So I hung her name on my bathroom mirror and every morning while I got ready for the day, I would mumble this sorry excuse for a prayer, "Oh yeah, and by the way, Lord, bring Mo to you." I said this lame prayer every day for the next four years.

Then, the most extraordinary chain of events started to happen. First, Mo got a job right across the street from where I lived. She was a teacher at a continuation school where she dealt with gang members and tough guys who had been kicked out of regular schools for carrying weapons and such. Mo was perfect for the job; those kids were actually scared of *her*. She didn't need a weapon; she had her mouth, remember? Mo asked me to watch her little boy, Matt, in the mornings, and, since he took a nice long morning nap, I said yes.

Every morning, Mo dropped Matt off on the way to work. When she picked him up at noon, he would sometimes still be sleeping, giving Mo and me time to sit and talk over tea or even lunch. During that year, Sheryl taught me how to connect and dive in with Mo; sort of like, "Houston, we're going in!"

When Mo was a bit "cross," I would imagine my arms positioned like a "cross" protecting me, and I would venture in where no man dared to go. As the darts were flying, I would ask her, "Mo, why did you just say that?" Instead of lashing back at her or running away, I would delve even deeper, asking questions like, "What's hurting inside of you right now that would make you react like that?" And amazingly, Mo would soften, sometimes start to cry, and tell me exactly what was hurting her. After about a year we started to become great friends. Is that a miracle or what? She wasn't interested in talking about the Lord and, if I tried, she

Mo and I became great friends.

changed the subject, so I just kept loving her and praying for her. My prayers got better, by the way.

The Catuara Sisters Quartet: (l-r) Liz, Adrienne, Kathleen, Mo

At the same time that I was concentrating on Mo, my youngest sister, Liz, began taking voice lessons from me. She was about sixteen and became proficient enough to join our group, making it a quartet.

We were thrilled to have Liz in the group because all of us loved her. She was an angel, our littlest lamb. The youngest of eight kids, Liz had wisdom beyond her years. Since she was a great listener, everyone went to little Liz with their problems. We nicknamed her "Lizzytish." I remember that when she was about four years old, she announced that her name was now "Sunnyflower," and, sure enough, if we didn't call her by that name, she wouldn't answer.

One night, after her voice lesson, Liz broke down and tearfully said, "Kathleen, I don't have all the answers! My classmates come to me with their problems. I try to point them to God, but I don't know enough about Him to tell them how to get His help!"

Well, she accepted Christ in my living room that very night. After Liz left, I looked up at God and said, "Lord? What's up with this? I pray everyday for Mo, and instead *Liz* comes to You? I didn't even pray for Liz. I don't get it." Liz and I started meeting once a week to study the Bible together.

Then, tragedy hit my family. About three months after Liz's conversion, I noticed that her skin color was different, a pale sort of yellow. I asked her if she was eating healthy, but Liz refused to eat any veggies. She called them the "V" word. I used to tease her and say that if she didn't start eating the "V" word that she would get the "C" word.

Then my mom told me that Liz had recently fainted and fallen out of her desk at school. After seeing a doctor, Liz was misdiagnosed with Epstein-Barr Syndrome, a very in-vogue disease for doctors to diagnose back then.

Let me tell you what the Lord did for me before everything hit. God is so kind and so gracious. He knew ahead exactly what I could and couldn't handle.

One night, shortly after Liz's fainting incident, the Lord woke me up in the middle of the night and said, "My daughter, I am going to take Liz to come live with me."

I was stunned, and replied, "Well...no...You can't have her," as if I owned her.

He then said ever so gently, "I want to pick *My* little Sunnyflower from *My* earthly garden, and bring her into *My* heavenly house, and put her on *My* mantle, so I can enjoy her close to Me." I remember bending over my living room couch, sobbing and begging, "Please don't take her! She's only a child. She just came to You."

And again He answered me, saying, "There is a bigger plan here that you don't know about. You have to trust Me."

"Please don't take her! She's only a child. She just came to You." And again He answered me, saying, "There is a bigger plan here that you don't know about. You have to trust Me."

It took me all night to come to grips with this. Steve heard me sobbing and got up to see what all of the ruckus was about. When I told him, he said, "Don't be ridiculous. Liz will be fine. Come to bed."

I didn't come to bed, and by six o'clock that morning, after wrestling with God all night, I finally had a sense of peace. I would need that peace to handle what was about to happen that very day.

Steve worked at the local hospital as an orderly. That afternoon, he called me from work, saying, "They just brought Liz in. She is having exploratory surgery in about an hour. You'd better get down here."

By the time I got to the hospital my whole family was huddled together in the middle of the lobby. I was about fifty feet away from them when my husband, Steve, walked out in his scrubs. Still in a huddle, they rushed toward him. The next scene will be etched in my memory forever. As Steve began telling them that Liz's body was filled with cancer, and that she only had months to live, he wasn't looking at my family—he was looking directly at me, in disbelief.

I remember what happened next like a slow motion movie. He had barely uttered the last words of this dreadful news when the entire family collapsed to the floor, like a teepee imploding. As the huddle was on its way down, Mo's hopeless face looked over at my peaceful face. She later told me that as she was going down, she thought, "Where did Kathleen get that peace? I want that." She hadn't seen me in a heap the night before, but, in God's great mercy and perfect timing, this moment between us started Maureen's journey to a personal relationship with Him.

Mo is a sharp cookie and had many questions about God that she wanted answered. She decided to meet with Jack's wife, Pat, and, for a solid year, went through the book of Romans and asked question after question. Then, one day, she simply announced to Pat, "Okay, I'm ready, let's do this."

Mo is now a dynamic Christian woman, a conference speaker, and an amazing, godly mother. Our friendship took on a whole new dimension, and we were finally able to freely talk about the Lord. Only God knows what it will take to bring a person to Him, and, four years earlier, He planted the first seed when He said, "Kathy, pray for Mo."

The next song on the CD is about loving the ones you think are not worth fighting for; those who are just too hard to love. Then I'll come back and finish my story about Liz.

Track#9: THIS ONE (HOPELESS FACE)

Verse 1
Just when I thought I can't love anymore,
I've prayed my last prayer I have cried my last tear.
You turned the knob and walked through a closed door,
The door to a heart that's been crippled with fear.
A heart that says love isn't worth all the agony.
Hoping and waiting and then,
There's no guarantee that you'll get what you're giving.
I can't go through that again.

Verse 2
But now that you're here and I'm looking at you,
A Voice in my head says, "Look deeper!"
It says, "Look for a heart that is aching for truth."
Then it tells me that this one's a keeper.
"This one's worth hurting for, hoping for, waiting for,
And when you are doubting keep going and pray.
The power of divine love can free you and teach you."

Chorus 1
"So you can bring hope.
So you can bring hope to a hopeless face."

Verse 3
We all have old demons that haunt us, they taunt us.
The past tries to grab us and hold us in place.
But the power of divine love will free you.

Chorus
So You can bring hope.
So you can bring hope, so you can bring hope
To a hopeless face.

Verse 4
You are worth risking for, weeping for, bleeding for.
You are as precious as gold in my sight.
Know you are loved so never give up.

Chorus
You can bring hope...Oh, you can bring hope,
You can bring hope...Oh, you can bring hope,
Oh, my beloved...You are worth the fight.

Liz

Liz's cancer bore far-reaching fruit; not just for Mo, but for my brother, Chris, as well. He accepted Christ soon after Maureen did. Besides my family, a steady stream of young people came to Liz's bedside during the next year, and she ministered to them in her sickness. Liz lived a year longer than the doctors predicted, and many of her friends came to the Lord during that time. She was so well loved, we counted five hundred cars at her funeral.

On her last birthday on earth, all of my sisters were gathered around her bedside and someone said, "Liz, don't you wish you had a million dollars to find a cure?" And this is what my nineteen-year-old, brand new Christian sister said, "You couldn't pay me a million dollars to not have cancer."

We all looked at her in shock. She said, "I was born for this. Without this cancer, I wouldn't have had the impact on all the students that I did. This was my ministry. This is the reason I was here."

I don't know that I could have said those words if I were in her shoes. The next song on the CD is called "Lizzytish, God's Littlest Lamb."

Track#10: LIZZYTISH, GOD'S LITTLEST LAMB

Verse 1
Lizzytish, the littlest lamb, how could you possibly know?
The lives you'd touch, that you'd do so much
In the hours before you had to go.
Sunnyflower, God's precious child, who could forget that smile?
You'd walk into a room, dispel all the gloom,
You who knew no guile.

Chorus
You didn't shake your fist at Him.
You didn't say, "Why me?"
Trapped in a broken body, longing to be free,
But you surrendered to His will.
You let Him use you weak and ill.
You said, "Here I am Lord, I will follow you."
"But other lambs are lost, Lord, let me lead them back to You."

Verse 2

You amazed us all when death came to call
And you said, "I just can't wait,
To run when He calls, not sick at all
And talk to Him face to face.
There'll be a big feast, all the hamburgers I could eat,
And I could eat them all day long.
And when I'm done I'll sit at His feet
And maybe I'll sing Him a song."

Verse 3

Lizzytish, the littlest lamb how could you possibly see
That it took your death to breathe new life into our family.
We all have grown since He took you home
To His heavenly house above.
He picked You out of His whole earthly garden
And set you on His mantle of love.

Chorus

You didn't shake your fist at Him.
You didn't say "Why me?"
And now He's saying, "Well done, little one.
No more death, you're finally free.
Now let me see that beautiful smile,
Won't you sit with me awhile?
You're home, little Sunnyflower.
Come and share the feast.
Be at peace, my littlest lamb.
I'm your Shepherd, come and sing for me."

Chapter 11: The "D" Word

etween my sister's death and my unhappy marriage—those were dark times. During the next ten years I worked full time to help Steve through medical school. To complete his schooling, we moved to Grenada in the West Indies and then to the East Coast. I left my successful business and even sold my beautiful walnut baby grand piano. (I had to throw that in and I'll tell you why later.) This move meant losing all of my support systems in Los Angeles. I said goodbye to my family, my friends, my church, and Sheryl. Steve and I moved thirteen times in the next ten years. I'm a pro at moving now, so if you need advice, call me! Everywhere we lived I found a good therapist and dragged myself and Steve to counseling. I'm a pro at that too. Call me.

Even with all that counseling, the marriage ended right after Steve finished medical school. I would love to tell you all of the sordid details, but, out of respect for Steve and obedience to the Lord, I can't. I was, however, thankful that we had no children.

When I realized that the marriage I had fought so long and hard for was finally over, I sunk into a deep depression. I didn't even recognize that it was depression. I just felt tired all the time and could barely function. Simple chores like laundry or paying the bills seemed overwhelming to me—I slept for days at a time.

I was living in Baltimore, working as a teacher and musical theater director at a very demanding private school in Washington, D.C. This was about an hour and a half commute for me—each way. And when I say demanding, that is definitely an understatement. Many of the students enrolled there were children of famous actors and senators. To give you an idea, I taught a Kennedy who arrived at school in a helicopter. I'm telling you this fun fact so that you can see just how demanding this gig was, and how professional I had to be; all the while sinking lower and lower into a dark emotional abyss. Steve and I had not been in Baltimore very long so I had no support system there yet. But I had to stay and finish out my contract.

After Steve and I separated, I would come home from school on Friday and sleep until Monday morning. My lowest point came when a well-meaning "Pastor" (I use that word loosely; he didn't have a church.) and his wife took me under their wings. I was so lonely that their friendship seemed like a breath of fresh air. I knew I needed to find a counselor and a good church, but I couldn't even get myself out of bed on the weekends. These two would come over and conduct church in my living room, with me in my pajamas. I was their only congregant. (Big red flag there.)

One Sunday morning, this couple started off our pajama service by saying, "Divorce is never God's will and you will never have a valid ministry if you are divorced. You will be living in a constant state of sin. No one will ever take you seriously and God can't use you or speak to you if you are in sin."

They implied that God was not a God of second chances. As they spoke, I shook my head thinking, "If this is really true, then I'm sunk." Even though they were sincere and meant well, those two Christians sent me into a deeper state of depression. Talk about the church shooting its own wounded. I thought, "Why even go on if the Lord isn't going to lead me or guide me?"

That couple also thought I should quit my job and follow Steve to wherever he moved and try to "get him back." When I told them that the Lord had specifically said to let him go, they questioned whether it was the Lord's voice I was hearing. Then they questioned whether I had *ever* heard the Lord's voice, saying it must have been Satan's voice I was hearing all of those years. I couldn't bear the picture they were painting of me; that I had messed up so badly even God could not redeem the situation. I was already in such a low emotional state that I couldn't battle the thoughts that began swimming around in my head: "Satan has been speaking to me all these years?"

As soon as they left my apartment, I began to contemplate ending this unredeemable life. That night, I decided to do it. I methodically ran through my mind the effects that killing myself would have on my family and friends back home. I made a mental list of everyone who would be affected, deciding that if I came across one person whose life would be completely ruined or devastated, I wouldn't do it.

...I began to contemplate ending this unredeemable life...."

As I starting writing the list, I thought, "My parents will be fine. They've already lost one child and they survived. Jack and Sheryl know what I've been through; they won't be surprised. Mo's got a good support system, she'll be fine." You can see how ridiculous my thought process was at this point.

As I was finishing up the list, I couldn't think of anyone who wouldn't understand. Now the question was, "Should I write a note? Yes, a note is good." As I was looking for paper and a pen to write the note, the name of one woman came to my mind: Karen Koeppl. She was a bright and beautiful colleague of mine that I had led to the Lord in New York shortly before we moved to Baltimore. I had been discipling her once a week and we had become good friends. "She will *not* understand," I thought. "She is a brand new Christian and this will rock her faith to the core." I had assured her over and over again that Jesus is the answer to all of life's problems.

I fell to the floor and choked out sob after sob because I realized that now I *had* to live. I cried out to God, "If this *is* You, don't make me go on without You." And then, remember that still small voice? Well, it wasn't still and it wasn't small—it was big. It had to be, so that I could hear it through my sobbing. God answered, "I never said you had to go on without Me. I never left. I'll never leave you. I'm here right now. Look at my face. *Look at my face.* It's Me. You know Me." And in my pain, I looked at His face and do you know what? I knew right then and there that it was Him. He hadn't left me at all. I realized, at that moment, that as long as I kept looking at His face, I could take one painful step at a time and make it through this miserable life. I could finish the race if I looked at His face.

He brought me to Hebrews 12:1-2 *"Run with endurance the race set before you fixing your eyes on Jesus the author and perfecter of faith who for the joy set before Him...* (that's me, I'm His joy,) *he endured the cross.*

> **God answered, "I never said you had to go on without Me. I never left. I'll never leave you...."**

Then He brought me to Jeremiah 29:11-13: *For I know the plans I have for you," declares the LORD, "plans for welfare and not for calamity...to give you a future and a hope. Then you will call upon me and come and pray to me, and I will listen to you. You will seek me and find me when you search for me with all your heart."*

And I love verse 29:14, *"And I will be found by you."*

Then, my gracious, loving Lord proceeded to give me a song. Ironically, to write this song I used the same pen and paper that just minutes before I was going to use to write a suicide note. The song He gave me was filled with hope for my future and a promise that He would indeed use me for His glory. It was one of those times when I could barely write fast enough to keep up with Him. By the time the song was done, I was actually laughing. (It had some funny parts in it.) Who but the "God of the Universe" could take a suicidal woman and in a matter of minutes have her laughing? Here's the song He used to do it.

Track#11: JESUS' FACE

Verse 1
Look into His eyes when you're running the race
Because right before He died, He looked into your face.
Like two in love who are willing to suffer
Because they only see each other.
The pain grows dim as I run to Him,
I can finish the race when I look at His face.

Chorus
Jesus' face, that's the place
To fix your eyes and mine.
You can run to the finish line
If you keep your eyes on Jesus' face.

Verse 2
Peter in the boat saw Jesus as his hope so he stepped out in faith.
But when he saw the raging seas, the water at his feet,
He turned his gaze. (Wrong move, Peter!)
When he lost sight of Jesus' face, well, he sank to a lower place.
Until Jesus took his hand only then could Peter stand
Amidst the storm as he looked at His face.

Chorus
Jesus' face, that's the place
To fix your eyes and mine.
You can walk on water,
You can run to the finish line
When you keep your eyes on Jesus' face.

Bridge
I can do anything through Christ who lives within me.
Greater things will you do than these...than these....

Verse 3
The apostles wondered how
They were gonna feed ten thousand hungry hands.
But they were busy looking down
At the fish on the ground
And what little they had.
But when they laid it at Jesus' feet,
You know that crowd had plenty to eat.
The job they had, it didn't look so bad
When they all looked up into Jesus' face.

Chorus
Jesus' face, that's the place
To fix your eyes and mine.
You can walk on water,
You can feed ten thousand,
You can run to the finish line,
If you keep your eyes,
You just keep your eyes,
Always keep your eyes
On Jesus' face...
On Jesus' face.

The Healing Years

Chapter Twelve:
God is My Husband

*F*rom this day forward, at probably the lowest point in my life, I found my soul mate in the "God of second chances," and, much to my surprise, life began to feel like a wondrous uphill ride. I guess one could say that this was the turning of the tide. God became my husband in the most unbelievable, tangible, and practical ways. Before this, I had tried hard to look at Him as a husband when my marriage felt husbandless. But, when the marriage was barely holding on by a shoe string, when I was desperately in need of Him, that's when God really stepped up to the plate. Reader, my new "Husband" met me at every level.

It was amazing. He acted the way a real husband would act: from helping me with major life decisions, to going with me on the most trivial errands, like picking out furniture. Normally I can pick out furniture myself, but, at that time, I was so stressed and frazzled that I needed someone to come alongside me. Since there was no one else around for the job, He volunteered. I can almost say that I'm glad to have gone through this painful season of my life because I experienced the God of the Universe caring for me like a devoted husband. He was my king again.

Okay. Bear with me for a moment. The next example may seem trivial, but, as women, we know that special encounters like these are worth mentioning. My apartment was empty except for a mattress, so I went to an estate sale. I needed everything: dishes, silverware; you name it, I needed it. I walked into the estate sale home and the inside looked like the yellow submarine. Everything was urine yellow: the walls, the furniture—everything. The furniture was actually really nice, but, come on, all yellow?

I thought, "This lady had really bad taste."

Cringing, I walked back out the door when my "Husband" said, "Go back in there and buy everything lock stock and barrel."

"Yellow? You want me to buy all yellow furniture?"

But, I knew my Lord's voice, so I went back in and asked how much the owners would take for everything. The price they quoted was so good I almost fainted. But then I thought, "They're probably desperate and can't unload anything because it's all yellow."

Later, I came back with a truck and movers. As they carried the furniture out the front door, to my amazement, I watched all of that yellow furniture turn white as it met the afternoon sunlight. It was *white* furniture that *looked* yellow because of the yellow walls. I jumped up and down like a maniac, crazy woman yelling, "It's white, it's white!" I danced all around the movers, who didn't know me from a hole in the head, yelling, "White, it's white!" The look on their faces was like, "Yeah, okay lady, so it's white." They thought I was off my rocker.

Oh, and the bonus? I wear clip-on earrings which are always so hard to find. (Only women could appreciate this.) The estate coordinator threw in fifty pairs of beautiful clip-on earrings for free...and, thank God, none of them were yellow. Furniture *and* earrings—what a Husband!

I still needed a hutch, and so I decided to hit some garage sales. I passed by a Sears store on the way and my "Husband" said, "Why don't you try Sears, Dear?" I couldn't afford a new hutch but thought, "With God, all things are possible." I walked in and discovered the most beautiful hutch I had ever seen. You know what it's like when something takes your breath away and is so "you" that it calls out your name. This hutch and I had an immediate attraction for each other, but the price...forget it.

I will never forget this. I reluctantly sauntered back to the escalator when my "Husband" said, "Kathy, go back and ask if they have a damaged one." So I went back and asked. The sales clerk looked at me in surprise and said, "Why…yes, we have one down in the warehouse for half price. Would you like to see it?"

"Uh… yeah."

A tiny piece of the glass shelving had chipped off. That was the damage. And I got it for half price! God knew this was a time in my life when I needed a little extra TLC.

May I give you one more example? And then it's back to the main story.

I wanted an old, comfy recliner. You know the kind I mean; a chair that most women would make their husbands throw away. I love to spend time with the Lord in an old chair like that, so I can put my Bible and notebook on the footrest that pops up in front. Now, mind you, this is not a need, it's a want. I'm perfectly fine having my quiet times in a regular chair like everybody else, so I dismissed the idea entirely.

I was driving into my apartment complex one day, when I saw a little piece of paper taped to a stop sign. As I passed by, my "Husband" said, "Turn around, and go back and check out that stop sign."

I peeked in and saw that the only items left in the apartment were a cozy brown recliner and six or seven beautiful large potted plants. Real ones!

It was cold outside and I complained. "You want me to get out of my car…blah blah blah." But I did, and the paper read "rummage sale;" however, the sign was old and the sale was over. At the very bottom of the paper, in really small print, were the words, "recliner for sale." So I thought, "Okay, I'll try it."

I drove to the address on the paper and saw two young guys carrying boxes out to a truck. They were, literally, ready to leave at any moment never to return again. As they walked by me, boxes in hand, the front door swung wide open. I peeked in and saw that the only items left in the apartment were a cozy brown recliner and six or seven beautiful large potted plants. Real ones! You know how much they cost!

I waited for the boys to come back and asked if the recliner was still for sale. They said yes—and the bonus? Wait for it, wait for it...I could have the chair *and* all of the plants for a whopping thirty-five dollars. I tried not to look too excited as they explained that I had to take the items immediately. The problem was I had no truck, and so I said, "Look, I only live a mile away and I can see you have room in your truck." I batted my eyes as femininely as I knew how and asked, "Do you think you could drop them off at my house on your way out of town?" They looked at each other for a moment and said, "Sure."

The two boys followed me to my apartment and carried the chair and all seven plants up a flight of stairs. For only thirty-five dollars, I ended up with a cozy recliner, plants, and even movers. What a God...what a Husband.

Okay, back to my story. I searched and finally found a counselor in Baltimore. He immediately put me on medication for depression. I didn't really want to take medication, because I'd always heard that it's more effective to deal with the cause of depression. But I called Sheryl and she explained to me that depression is debilitating and sometimes disorienting, making it difficult for a person to think clearly. Depression is somewhat like being sick; you can't write a term paper with a high fever or a bad flu. The medicine can return your body to a state in which you function more normally, and avoid creating a new set of problems, such as being fired from your job or becoming homeless.

> *I've learned that there are three categories of people who suffer from depression.*

I've since learned that there are three categories of people who suffer from depression. The first contains people with severe depression who need the medication in order to avoid creating a new set of problems in their lives. If these individuals do not take medications, the consequences could be destructive to themselves and their families. The hope here is that these hurting people will face their internal pain, as the medications reduce their distress to a tolerable level. I was in this first category. I took medication for about a year which really helped me function through the worst times.

The second category includes people with mild to moderate depression who use medication as an escape in an attempt to avoid dealing with the painful internal feelings they are experiencing. Instead of facing this pain, they often self-medicate with alcohol, drugs or other addictions. This approach can also have long-lasting and dangerous consequences.

The third category involves those with mild to moderate depression who do not want to depend on medications or use them to avoid facing their inner pain. They have the courage to face their feelings head on without unnecessary dependency on substances.

By the end of that year, I finished out my contract at the school and the headmaster asked me to stay on permanently. It seemed the logical thing to do. I was making great money in a secure job and was just starting to build some really good friendships at a new church I was attending. But, I missed California, my family, and my old friends. I felt the Lord telling me it was time to go home so I decided to look for a teaching position in Los Angeles. At the same time, the headmaster had given me a deadline to make an official decision by the third Saturday in May.

A couple of schools in Hollywood flew me out for interviews but, when I prayed about which job to take, God said, "Wait." Remember when He told me to wait on the medical decision? Well, I'd learned that "wait" means wait. Because the two schools were rivals, and each one thought I was waiting because the other was counter-offering (That wasn't the case, God just said not to accept either job yet), they both kept offering me more money and more perks. One of these perks included moving expenses which was crucial since I had no money to pay for a move across the country. To top it off, both schools offered me free housing. Anyone would have been thrilled.

That third Saturday in May was so miraculous that it reminded me of the morning I walked into the doctor's office at UCLA.

Here's what happened:

I had until midnight to email the headmaster with my final decision. At 9:30 in the morning I read in James, *"If anyone lacks wisdom let Him ask of God who gives generously without reproach and it will be given to Him."* (James 1:5).

So I asked my Husband, "Which school should I choose?"

"Neither."

"Okay, then You must want me to stay in Baltimore."

"No."

"Lord, why are you saying no to everything?" But then this thought came to me.

"Kathy, what have you always wanted to do more than anything else?"

Jim and Denise

I thought for a moment and said, "Work at a church." I'd always dreamed of doing that. Then I looked at my watch and said to the Lord, "Okay, Lord. How am I going to get a church job, money to move, *and* a place to live in just fourteen-and-a-half hours? Because if those three things don't happen by midnight, then I'm going to say yes to my headmaster."

Then Lord said, "Watch Me. Call Denise."

Denise worked at a large church east of Los Angeles that had the most amazing worship center, a great musical theater department, and a revolving stage. I would have called her right away, but it was only six thirty in the morning her time. And so I waited. Boy, was that a long morning! We chatted for bit and as I was about to hang up, she said, "Kathy, did you call me for any specific reason?"

"Well, I sort of need a job."

"Isn't that interesting? The Worship Pastor at my church is looking for someone."

Then I heard myself say, "Yeah...but...I sort of...need one by midnight tonight."

She didn't even flinch. I love that woman! She said, "Let me call you back."

After waiting all afternoon, Denise's worship Pastor, Bill Risinger, called me and gave me an interview over the phone. He said, "You come highly recommended by Denise. We trust her, you're hired."

Over the phone! Who hires anyone over the phone? What church hires a *divorced* woman over the phone? I had my first, second, and final interview in a matter of minutes, never having the chance to negotiate. When I asked about the salary, Bill told me the salary was only half of what I was making at the school. I hesitated for a moment, and then he quickly added, "but I have six voice students ready for you as soon as you get here and plenty more where they came from."

Okay, that was Miracle #1. One down, two to go.

Bill continued, asking, "So, when can you be here?"

"Uh...um...can I get back to you on that?" I had no clue how I was going to get there. He wasn't offering me a moving package like the schools and it costs thousands of dollars to move across country.

By now the time was 4:30 pm. "Seven and a half hours to go, God," I said.

I read in the book of Ruth how Boaz laid his cloak over her as a promise to take care of her and meet her needs. Ruth called him her kinsman redeemer.

"Okay, Lord, You are my kinsman redeemer and I need another miracle."

At 5:00 pm Mo called me out of the blue. I told her about the job and she said, "Well isn't this a coincidence? The State of California just bought my house for a ridiculously huge amount of money to put a freeway through our backyard. Mike and I are so thankful to the Lord that we want to send you a portion of what we made so that you can move home."

It took me a moment to let that sink in and then I was speechless (which by the way, doesn't happen very often). My sister said, "Kathleen, Kathleen, are still there?"

"Yeeessss!" I choked out.

That was Miracle #2; two down, one to go.

By this time it was 6:00 pm and I still needed a place to live.

I reminded the Lord, "Only six hours left until midnight!" as if He needed reminding. Isn't this exciting? By now, I'm like, "Bring it on Boaz!" My faith was sky high.

The hours ticked by and finally, at 11:30 pm, Denise called.

"Hey, do you want to come live at our house until you get on your feet?" she asked.

"Do I!"

This was the second time in my life that a Christian couple let me live with them, rent free, when I really needed it.

And that was Miracle #3; all three in a matter of hours.

The time was exactly 11:55 pm when I finished the email to my headmaster stating that I would not be returning in the fall. Isn't God amazing? This is the song the Lord gave me as I sat there at midnight in awe of what my kinsman redeemer had just done for me.

Track #12: RUTH'S SONG (LAY YOUR CLOAK OVER ME)

Chorus
Lay your cloak over me, Oh Lord. Lay your cloak over me.
My Kinsmen Redeemer, lay your cloak over me.
Will you take care of me, Oh Lord?
And the future I can't see?
I am laying at your feet where the two of us can meet.
Lay your cloak over me. Lay your cloak over me.

Verse
Like a wife who has loved but been rejected,
Are you battered, abused or just neglected?
Do you think there's no hope?
You're at the end of your rope where faith is tested.
Well there's a man out there who'll take you into his care.
His name is Jesus.
He loves you so much more than you've been loved before.
Why don't you go to Him…and say…

Chorus
Lay your cloak over me, Oh Lord.
Lay your cloak over me.
My Kinsmen Redeemer, lay your cloak over me.
Will you take care of me, Oh Lord?
And the future I can't see?
I am laying at your feet where the two of us can meet.
Lay your cloak over me.
I am laying at your feet every need that I can't meet.
Lay your cloak over me. Lay your cloak over me.

Chapter Thirteen: Things Are Looking Up

*H*ow can I describe the next four years: chocolate on a brownie, Kool-Aid in a desert, ointment on a wound. The next four years at Victoria Community Church was a time of deep healing and restoration. I thrived and blossomed in my new job, and the best part was…I got to see Denise at work and at home.

The church offered a divorce recovery class that really helped me to heal. I learned in that class that during a divorce you may need to tell your friends not to expect as much from you interpersonally. They may need to be the "givers" until your time of healing is past; but, if your friends can be patient, they will not be on the giving end forever. Those who are your true friends will understand this dilemma and stick around for the long haul.

I loved how the class explained the reason for this interpersonal dynamic.

We all have four energy quadrants:

Physical 25%

Emotional 25%

Spiritual 25%

Mental 25%

When going through a divorce, you expend 85 percent of your emotional energy just to survive each day. That leaves 15 percent to be divided amongst the other three quadrants or only five percent each. This concept is important to understand so that you are not too hard on yourself when exhaustion immobilizes you. *Give Yourself a Break!* Try to lower your stressors as much as you can, and be good to yourself during that time.

I can't tell you how nice it was to be back with old friends who knew my history so that I didn't have to explain myself or my situation a million times! They were the kind of friends who gave to me when I couldn't give back. Once I had become financially established, Denise and Jim dropped me out of the nest to fly on my own. I moved out and bought a house in Riverside.

By then, Leslie, one of the music secretaries at the church, had become a good friend. She was also one of those rare people who knew what you needed before you even told her. One morning, I let drop the fact that I had stacks of bills and important receipts piled up so high on my bedroom floor that they reached the top of my mattress. I only told her because I thought it was funny. But Leslie and her husband showed up the next Saturday morning and, while he did all of my yard work, she filed all of my receipts. There were hours and hours worth of receipts to file and she wouldn't even let me help her. She said, "Just sit there and talk to me." That was just like her. What a great example of giving without expecting anything in return.

I also learned that rebound dating is dangerous because you haven't had sufficient time to heal and you aren't thinking with full mental clarity. A counselor once told me that for every four years you were married, it takes one year to recover from a divorce. I did not heed those words and dated foolishly. Even with God as my Husband, I still battled looking to men for approval. Sometimes I still struggle in this area.

Believe it or not, my family was a real blessing to me during this time of healing. While I was gone all those years, they went through some significant changes too. Many of my siblings went to counseling and, with the help of Sheryl, came to me individually asking my forgiveness for how they had treated me while we were growing up. Another big change that happened while I was gone was the fact that my brother, Chris, started attending Jack's church and met and married his daughter, Jill. Like Sheryl, Jill was a marriage and family counselor, and now my family is permanently linked to Jack's. What a blessing!

God began to make up for all of the years the locusts had eaten. The inner pain I was so accustomed to, that I lived with every day, was becoming a distant memory. The old Kathy was re-emerging.

At forty years old, I had just bought my first house and I was ecstatic. I remember standing in the middle of my new empty house, dancing around like a fairy princess. The only item I had brought into the house so far was a baby grand piano. If you recall, I had sold my walnut baby grand to help pay for Steve's schooling. To a musician whose livelihood is music, that was a huge sacrifice, and I had promised myself the first thing I would do when I got established was buy another baby grand. I didn't care if I had to eat beans the rest of my life, I was going to replace that baby grand.

This is funny: I bought the piano on credit—excited that my payments were only going to be $107 a month. I didn't read the fine print on the contract until someone finally brought it to my attention that I was actually paying $100 in interest and $7 toward the principle. I would have been making payments on that piano for the rest of my life. I re-financed.

Some single gals moved in with me and we had a great time. It felt just like old times. The cloud was lifting and I felt like shouting with joy from the rooftops. The next song on the CD is taken straight out of scripture. I wrote a tune to Isaiah 54: 1-3 during one of my "bursting with joy" moments. We have fun with this one during the conference because I invite a few of the ladies to come up and play Jewish-type instruments. I have a shofar, a horn that looks like a giant tusk, that the women can barely get a sound out of…it's hilarious to watch!

Track#13: SHOUT FOR JOY

Shout for joy oh barren woman, you who have born no child.
Break forth into singing and dancing,
Joyfully shout out loud.
For the sons of the desolate ones will be more
Than the sons of the women who wed says the Lord.
Expand the land where your tents are placed.
Enlarge the drapes of your dwelling place.
Lengthen your pegs, strengthen your cords.
You will spread to the right and the left says the Lord
And your children will rule over nations.
This is the song of salvation.

>   *Shout for joy oh barren woman, you who have born no child.*
>   *Break forth into singing and dancing,*
>   *Joyfully shout out loud.*
>   *For the sons of the desolate ones will be more*
>   *Than the sons of the women who wed says the Lord.*
>   *Expand the land where your tents are placed.*
>   *Enlarge the drapes of your dwelling place.*
>   *Lengthen your pegs, strengthen your cords.*
>   *You will spread to the right and the left says the Lord*
>   *And your children will rule over nations.*
>   *This is the song of salvation.*
>   *Your children will rule over nations.*
>   *This is the song of salvation.*

The Fruitful Years

Chapter Fourteen:
Songs During the Fruitful Years

I call those years at the church the "fruitful years" because the Lord gave me song after song during that time. One of my jobs at the church was to write songs that complimented the Pastor's sermons. Often the Lord would wake me up at 4:00 in the morning and say, "Go to the piano. I've got one for you!" To this day, I don't understand why He had to wake me up that early. What was wrong with 6:00 or 7:00 or even 9:00 in the morning? I guess I'll find out in heaven.

When people would come up to me after the services and share that the Lord used one of my songs to encourage or convict them, I would say under my breath, "Take *that,* Satan! I *do* have a ministry. God *is* using me—a divorced woman. And God *is* a God of second chances. So there! *plhhh*!!!!"

I'd like to share a few of those songs with you before I begin the final chapter of my story.

Song #14 on the CD is called, "Lookin' Back." I based the song on a sermon called "Afraid to Go Forward." That sermon hit home with me because I was afraid to do these conferences, arguing with God for more than ten years. I kept telling Him He had the wrong gal!

One morning I was hiking up a very steep mountain when I reached a plateau about halfway to the top. Huffing and puffing, I looked ahead of me deciding that I couldn't possibly make it to the top after all. When I turned around and saw that the distance I had already come was about the same distance I still had left to go, I thought, "You made it up *this* far, Kathy, you can make it up *that* far!" Looking back from where I'd been from the place I was standing in gave me the confidence to get to where I was going. The next morning at 4:00 am the Lord gave me this song.

Track#14: LOOKIN' BACK

Chorus
Lookin' back at where you've been
From the place you're standing in
Will give you faith to get you where you're goin'.
Don't you see you've come so far.
Take a look at where you are.
Nothin's gonna stop you now get goin.'

Verse 1
God's people in the desert
Came right to the edge of the land.
God told them all to enter
'Cause He'd given it into their hands.
But they forgot who God was,
What He'd done, where they'd been, how they got there.
Instead they chose to cower, insulting His great power.
Israel's finest hour!
They had to turn back when they tried to attack
Then they grumbled and said, "This is not fair!"

Chorus
Lookin' back at where you've been
From the place you're standing in
Will give you faith to get you where you're goin'.
Don't you see you've come so far.
Take a look at where you are.
Nothin's gonna stop you now get goin'.

Verse 2
The Lord says to remember over and over again
The mercies He's bestowed on us

In spite of our blindness and sin.
Don't forget the miracle that He'd even call you His child.
He chooses who He uses.
The one who snoozes, loses.
The wise ones He confuses.
Open your eyes, do you see any pride?
He is calling the meek and the mild.

Chorus
Lookin' back at where you've been
From the place you're standing in
Will give you faith to get you where you're goin'.
Don't you see you've come so far.
Take a look at where you are.
Nothin's gonna stop you now get goin'.
Pull up your boot straps and get goin'.
Get goin'! Get goin'!
   (Ad lib)

~~~

How many of you have ever turned your back for a second and lost track of your child in a mall or large public place? It's a horrible feeling and one you never forget. My senior pastor asked me to write a Mother's Day song comparing a mother's love to God's love for his lost children. I wrote a melody line but cried every time I tried to sing the song in public. I finally made it into a skit instead so that I wouldn't have to sing it.

Track#15: I JUST COULDN'T SAY NO!

I was at the mall with my little boy.
I was looking at shoes and getting annoyed.
He kept putting his Pooh Bear onto the floor
Then drop kicking it across the store.
I finally found the right pair to try on,
But when I turned around…my son was gone.

I tried to stay calm as I looked everywhere,
then I saw it, alone...his little Pooh Bear.

Every sound around me a muffled blur,
As if in slow motion I heard my own words.
"My child is lost, he's been taken," I cried,
"Just a minute ago he was here at my side."
I called out his name again and again
But he didn't answer me....So then
I grabbed hold of the salesclerks just standing around.
"Will you help me," I pleaded, "until he is found?"
And at that moment the whole world disappeared.
They shared only one purpose, help this woman in tears.
They saw in my eyes that I wouldn't let go,
So they stopped what they were doing,
They just couldn't say no.

As everyone searched every inch of that store,
As if I could bargain, I said to the Lord,
"If you return him to me, I'll come back to you too.
I'll obey every word; I'll do anything for you."
Suddenly, a salesclerk shouted these words.
No sweeter words have I ever heard!
"I found him! I found him! I knew right where to look.
He was at Pooh's corner bookstore, He was reading a book."
I can't even tell you the cheers and the joy
That rang out in that mall when I found my lost boy.

That night I thanked God I could still tuck him in.
And here's where my story really begins.
As I mulled over the events of that day,
The Lord spoke to me in His soft gentle way.
"You said you'd return, but will you obey?
I have a job for you starting today."

Every sound around me a muffled blur,
As if in slow motion I heard my Lord's words.
"My children are lost, they've been taken," He cried,
"I long to have them all here at my side.
I've called out their names again and again
But they just don't answer me" and then,
He grabbed hold of my heart, as I knelt on the ground.
"Will you help me?" He pleaded, "until they are found?"
And at that moment the whole world disappeared.
We shared only one purpose and that purpose was clear.
I saw in His eyes that He wouldn't let go.
I stopped what I was doing, I just couldn't say no.

~~~

The next track on the CD is a song I wrote for a Christmas service. The sermon was called "What will you do about Jesus?" I call this piece a "skong" because it is a skit and a song combined. Forgive me, Daniel Webster! I love the message in this one because it requires an answer from the hearers.

Track#16: WHAT WILL YOU DO ABOUT JESUS?

Joseph: This is the *perfect* Gift! My son is going to love this wooden wagon!

As soon as he gets old enough he can put all of his little toys in it. Once I get the wheels on he can pull it around with him just like Daddy's big cart in the woodshop.

Where are those nails? Oh, here they are. It's got to be sturdy because this cart could be in the family for generations. Jesus will probably get married, have children of his own and then pass it down to his children and his children's children. Why, this little cart might even be famous some day. People will say, "This is the gift that Joseph made for King Jesus when he was just an infant."

Imagine that, wood and nails going down in history!
This is the perfect gift!

Verse 1
Somewhere far away,
Under a star there lay,
A baby boy named Jesus.
Only a few, people knew
What He came to do,
That He came to free us.
But sin dulls the senses,
The eyes can't see.
The ears can't hear what he's saying.
The heart is hard,
The mind confused.
The spirit is dead.
No souls are praying.

Verse 2
Not so far away,
From where you stand today,
A broken place needs Jesus.
They don't know
Which way to go,
To find some rest,
Unless we tell them.
But sin dulls the senses,
The eyes can't see.
The ears can't hear what he's saying.
The heart is hard,
The mind confused.
The spirit is dead.
No souls are praying.

Chorus
So, what will you do about Jesus?
'Cause here's what He did about you.
He left his own father, his throne above,
He came because He loves you.

He took all the blame, bore all the pain,
For every name that calls him.

> *What will you do about Jesus?*
> *'Cause here's what He did about you.*
> *He took on your sin so your eyes could see,*
> *So your ears could hear what He's saying.*
> *He'll give you a new heart that He can use*
> *To wake the dead into living.*

So what will you do about Jesus?
What will you do about him?
Open your heart and let him in,
Let him begin to love you.
What will you do? What will you do?
Will you?
Love him.

~~~

"Oh Holy Night" is a classic Christmas carol describing the night Jesus was born. The Lord gave me the idea to wrap another song around it describing the night Jesus died. I call the duet "Two Nights" and churches all over the U.S. sing it at Christmastime. If you didn't notice already, the picture on the front and back covers of this book depicts those two monumental nights. Thank you Jessica Willet for your beautiful artwork.

This song stands out because it links the two most important nights in history.

Track#17: TWO NIGHTS

Oh Holy Night
by John S. Dwight and Adolphe Adam

Verse 1
Oh Holy Night, the stars are brightly shining.
It is the night of our dear Savior's birth.
Long lay the world in sin and error pining
Till He appeared and the soul felt its worth.
A thrill of hope the weary world rejoices
For yonder breaks a new and glorious morn.
Fall on your knees, oh hear the angel's voices.
Oh night divine, oh night when Christ was born.
Oh night divine, oh night, oh night divine.

> The Night He Died
> by Kathy Ashdown
>
> Verse 2
> *The night He died the world stood still and dark,*
> *The sky was black*
> *On the night of my dear Savior's death, He died for me.*
> *Upon that tree, the world set free from sin.*
> *He finally came to conquer death and my soul found rebirth.*
> *A thrill of hope as my weary soul rejoices,*
> *So long He's waited for you to be reborn.*
> *Oh! I fall, I fall on my knees and I weep.*
> *I hear my Savior's voice on the night He died.*
> *Oh it thundered on the night the temple veil was torn.*
> *He said, "Tonight, child, you shall be with me in paradise.*
> *Oh, tonight you're mine."*

Now, Dear Reader. Are you ready? Let's move on to the last chapter.

The Happy Years

Chapter Fifteen: Scott and Kathy

*A*t last we have come to the final chapter of my story. On the last evening of every PJs Women's Conference, my husband, Scott, joins me as we both describe how we met. Talk about a popcorn story! You definitely need to put this book down right now and go pop up a big tub of some yummy popcorn. But come right back,

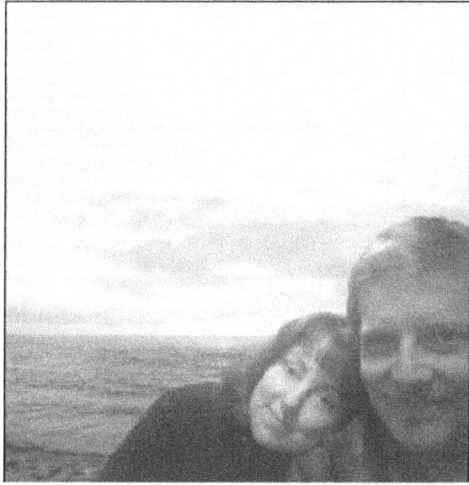

Kathy and Dr. Scott

because this story is like watching a movie. I call this season in my life the happy years and I'm still in them. I want you to see what a difference a healthy marriage makes. Letting God choose a man for me was the best decision I ever made and I'm still reaping the benefits. This is going to be a fun chapter because my husband Scott will tell his side of the story too. We're both so excited to tell you!

Okay, I'll start.

KATHY: I noticed a few of my close girlfriends losing weight, tanning, and suddenly filling up their social calendars. They went from couch potatoes to social butterflies and I had to know why. When I inquired about this phenomenon, all three said, "Christian online dating." I used to joke that those websites reminded me of a modern day version of an old Italian "verbal" grapevine; a mama telling another mama in a nearby town that her single daughter was available, boasting about her daughter's beautiful attributes, and listing out on each finger what the mama was looking for in a husband for her precious jewel. I always said that online dating sites were faster and more efficient, but I never dreamed I would actually join one, let alone *advocate* one.

SCOTT: I was skeptical and thought online dating was a bad idea from the get go. I would never have investigated it if a friend of mine hadn't told me about her experiences. She piqued my curiosity. I had dated several women, but couldn't seem to find what I was looking for. I developed a list of twelve qualities necessary for the woman I was going to be with. At the most, I only found one or two of these qualities in the women I was seeing.

KATHY: I dated a bit, but couldn't find a man with a personality stronger than mine. I thought maybe I could find a strong man online, but I decided to pray about it first. God said, "Absolutely not!" so I tabled the idea all together. Here's where the story gets good!

About a year after that prayer, I was driving in my car, minding my own business, when all of a sudden the Lord said, "Kathy, it's time. I want to you try the online dating."

I was shocked! "You said no before! Well, I guess You have the right to change your mind, after all, You *are* God."

He answered, "You weren't ready. You needed more time to heal."

That made sense. But still, this is a *big* change of mind and I wanted to be certain it *was* His voice I was hearing so I said, "Okay, Lord, please confirm your will to me. I'm talking about a baseball bat over the head kind of confirmation."

SCOTT: I love how God speaks to you.

KATHY: The next morning when I walked into work, my secretary said, "Kathy, Bill is waiting in his office. He wants to see you immediately."

If you recall, Bill was my boss at the church. When I walked into his office he said, "Shut the door."

I thought, "Uh oh, this is serious." Then, when I saw tears in his eyes, I panicked. "Oh, I am *so* fired. I probably said something stupid to my team that I can never take back." (Remember... strong personality.)

This is what Bill said: "Kathy, I was driving out to Orange County yesterday when I heard a well known Christian organization on the radio advocating an online dating site. I thought, 'No way would I ever let *my* daughter do that.' No sooner had that thought entered my mind when the Lord spoke to me and said, 'I want you to tell Kathy to try online dating.'"

Now, Reader, you must understand my boss. Bill did not meddle in his employees' dating affairs. He had good work ethics and always stayed focused on the worship ministry, so this was very embarrassing for him, to say the least.

Bill went on to say, "I just couldn't believe my ears, so I mulled over it all day. On the way back from Orange County the same program aired again and this time the Lord said, 'Are you going to obey me?'"

So, with his face beet red, Bill announced, "I'm supposed to tell you to do the online dating thing."

Well, you talk about a baseball bat! That was a home run!!

I just stood there in utter amazement. Then, I told Bill that the Lord had spoken to me at the same hour He had spoken to him. We both cried.

I could hardly wait for my work day to end! I raced home and eventually found a site called ChristianMingle.com.

SCOTT: God's timing is amazing! Kathy and I both went on the site within a few days of each other. "Christian Mingle" was actually a pretty decent site. The questions they asked about your religious beliefs were worded in such a way that you could tell if someone was faking their answers, making it pretty easy to see a person's real spiritual maturity. Again, I was skeptical, but felt I should at least give it a shot. Not really believing anything would come of it, I wrote my answers as honestly and authentically as I could.

KATHY: Okay...*that's* an understatement. Scott wrote things like, "I don't need a woman who thinks she is my Holy Spirit. I already have one, thank you very much."

I'll share my response to *that* one in a minute. My brother, Joey, took some pictures of me out on his front lawn that looked so beautiful I wanted to cut out one of the faces and glue it to my face permanently. (Thank God for Photoshop!) I posted the pictures onto the site and filled out the personal profile page. The next day, I was shocked to receive 275 hits. (For us dinosaurs who don't have a thorough knowledge of computer slang, a "hit" is a response to your page.)

There was no way I could possibly respond to that many emails, so I made a decision to go through and delete (without even opening) every email that had no picture. I had heard stories of guys showing up with no teeth or no fingers. I wanted to see all appendages!

I also decided to delete any email whose sender lived beyond two hours away because I certainly did *not* want to start a sappy long distance relationship. I stayed up until midnight that night deleting and deleting and deleting...until...I saw "Scootera." I *almost* deleted him because there was no picture and he was from Oregon, a thousand miles away. But his comment stopped me.

SCOTT: The "hits" Kathy is referring to are actually what the site calls a Smile; a one line, preset response that I could choose from to send her. Once she received a Smile, she could look at my profile without actually having to communicate with me. If she didn't accept the Smile, then...that's it...goodbye.

KATHY: What stopped me short was Scott's choice of Smiles. All the other guys sent Smiles about themselves, but Scott sent one about me. How rare is that? He chose one that acknowledged my passion for life. I only opened his profile because I rationalized to myself, "Well, I won't date the guy, but maybe I'll discover a good friend in Oregon."

When I opened his profile my heart started beating right out of my pink sweater! He was almost too good to be true. Scott had been a pastor, played guitar, and worked with youth. But the "cha-ching" moment was when I saw the word "psychologist." Free counseling for the rest of my life? Wow! I would have been thrilled with just one out of those four descriptions.

Then I went on to read that Scott's favorite Bible passage was John 15. I couldn't believe it, John 15 was the chapter I based my whole Christian walk on. I kept thinking, "This guy gets it, he *really* gets it!" What sealed the deal was Scott's line about not needing a Holy Spirit wife. Anyone else would have read that and said, "Man, this guy's got baggage." But not me, I said, "Finally, a man I can't manipulate and control." I was smitten. Since there was no picture of him I guess you could say it was love at first "site."

SCOTT: On my end, I was just shaking my head in amazement at how much we had in common. I was shocked at how many of Kathy's qualities were on my list. In fact, she met all twelve within two or three days of getting to know her. I was just amazed. So much was going right with Kathy that at times I thought it was too good to be true. Plus, those pictures were the most beautiful I had ever seen.

I paid him to say that!

KATHY: I paid him to say that.

SCOTT: We started talking on the phone for about two or three hours a night and, sometimes six to eight hours per day on the weekends.

KATHY: If you compared the amount of time we talked to a typical date that included dinner and a movie, we probably talked a total of four dates in one phone call.

SCOTT: We even had movie dates over the phone. Kathy and I would both rent the same movie like "Princess Bride," grab some popcorn and watch it at the same time. That was fun.

KATHY: They weren't always fun though. Sometimes our phone conversations sounded more like interrogations because we were both so hurt from our past. We kept looking for some kind of red flag. Scott would make up scenarios like, "What if you really wanted to buy a certain couch and I thought we should wait? What would you do?" I would ask him questions like, "What would you do if I gained ten pounds?"

SCOTT: Within about two weeks, we both realized we needed to meet in person. So I decided to fly down to L.A.

KATHY: I hate to even admit this, but I knew Scott was "the one" after only two weeks. I told him I loved him over the phone before I ever saw his face in person. I just knew it was God this time because I was listening closely to His Holy Spirit.

SCOTT: I had to wait to tell her I loved her out of sheer principle. I wanted to say it too, but I refused to do it until I met her face to face. Excited to take the next step, I flew down to Los Angeles to see her. She had instructed me to meet her at the bottom of an escalator outside the airport gate where I would signal her with this crazy sort of "duck" wave so she would recognize me. I will never forget that day. It is probably the single most nerve-wracking moment in my life—I would finally meet her face to face! I was on the escalator scanning the crowd of people who were eagerly looking up to find their loved ones and there I was doing this idiotic hand signal and…no one signaled back. For a moment I panicked thinking, "This *was* too good to be true after all; she's changed her mind." I went into the airport bathroom and looked in the mirror saying, "Calm down, Scott! Just calm down!"

KATHY: Poor guy! I was late because, struck with a case of uncontrollable nervousness, I took the wrong entrance ramp onto the freeway and ended up driving half an hour in the wrong direction. I didn't even realize it until I saw signs for Redlands, and by then I was *really* late!

SCOTT: I came out of the bathroom and, by this time, the crowd was gone. So now I was standing all alone with my brief case at the bottom of the escalators.

KATHY: When I got to the airport I broke into a full run… heels and all. As I quickly approached the escalators, I saw Scott, standing with his back to me, looking mighty good from behind. I prayed, "Oh Lord, let that be him!" (Scott hates when I say that publicly but…too bad.) And it was! Yippee!

SCOTT: We just hugged and cried for about five minutes looking deep into each other's eyes. We both felt like we were finally home. Then I took Kathy's hand and we walked out to her car and kissed for a long time. Yippee!

KATHY: He finally said he loved me.

SCOTT: Yep.

KATHY: Wait until you hear this! Scott and I went to eat lunch at Black Angus restaurant where Mo had given me discount coupons.

That should have tipped me off right there. As we sat gazing into each other's eyes, a strange person walked by our table wearing a Groucho Marx mustache, fake nose and eyeglasses. I didn't think much of it until that weird person plopped right down at our table. It was Mo. She was worried Scott might be some kind of kidnapper or something so she planned on watching us from a table in the back of the restaurant. Only Mo! She actually phoned Scott's office in Portland to see if he was legit. Gotta love her!

Scott passes the Spaghetti Night test.

SCOTT: I met Kathy's family and I guess I passed the Wednesday night spaghetti test.

KATHY: Even though I said I never would, we dated long distance, flying up and down from Portland to L.A. We dated for only three short months before Scott decided to pick out a ring. I was positive he was going to ask me on Thanksgiving because I saw the ring being delivered to his house.

SCOTT: But when I realized Kathy might be expecting it, I decided to wait to surprise her.

KATHY: Again, he won't be controlled! I went back to L.A. with no ring on my finger and I was a very unhappy girl.

SCOTT: The next week, I flew out to L.A. and we decided to go to Disneyland. Kathy and I were eating at the Blue Bayou Restaurant inside the park and the atmosphere was very romantic. Kathy got up from the table to watch the Pirates of the Caribbean boats go by, and I thought, "This is the moment! It's got to be now!"

The night we were engaged

KATHY: Ever since I was a kid, I looked longingly from inside those pirate boats at the people eating in the Blue Bayou restaurant and thought, "Someday I'm going to make enough money to eat there!" I was actually silently taunting those boats saying, "You're out there and I'm in here. Na na na na, Na na," when Scott walked up behind me.

SCOTT: I pretended like I had a terrible headache and asked if she could get my aspirin bottle opened.

KATHY: As I opened up the bottle, there was the ring. Scott was miraculously all better as he took my hands in his and recited the most beautiful marriage proposal.

SCOTT: My friend, Ken, said I should have brought a fake ring and, just as Kathy and I were speeding down the waterfall on the Pirates ride, I should have pulled out the fake ring and accidentally let it go flying out of the boat.

KATHY: I know with absolute certainty that had I seen you drop that ring I would have pushed you out of the boat to go find it.

SCOTT: I believe you.

KATHY: I danced out of that restaurant showing my ring to any stranger who would stop long enough to look. There I was, a forty-something year old woman, singing at the top of my lungs, "I'm getting married, I'm getting married!"

SCOTT: Kathy called her family immediately and they pretty much dropped what they were doing to meet us at Mimi's café. When we walked in the door of the restaurant we found that her family had already decorated the place with balloons and flowers.

KATHY: They work fast.

SCOTT: I think they were really glad to see Kathy so happy after all she had been through. In true Italian form, Mo came up to me and said firmly, "Welcome to the family, Scott. You hurt her, we'll kill you."

KATHY: Don't mess with us!

SCOTT: Even though I really didn't have to, I asked Kathy's dad for her hand in marriage. Joe knew I played competitive golf in college, so he told me I could marry her if I helped him gain ten more yards off the tee.

KATHY: Our plan was to wait until the summer to marry but my pastor advised us not to wait that long which really surprised me. I usually tell the women I mentor to wait at least one year before they say "yes" because, let's face it, men usually put their best foot forward for about a year. When women come to me for advice about this I've been known to literally plug my ears and say, "Come back and talk to me after you've known him for at least a year."

Scott and Kathy at their wedding reception

Now, I was being counseled *not* to wait. The pastor felt at our age, with both of us certain this was of God, that waiting could bring along too much temptation. It's not like we were in our twenties. We both knew this was it.

SCOTT: We met in September, got engaged in November and were married six months later in February. The rest is history.

KATHY: So that's how we met. Thanks, Scott, for sharing this chapter with me!

SCOTT: My pleasure.

~~~

To close, I would like to give you, the reader, a taste of what it's been like being married to "Mr. Right." I pray that this list of ten points will encourage you to hope for God's best and challenge you to wait for God's movement when seeking a mate.

1. There is no dark emotional cloud hovering over my home. Instead, I hear singing when I walk in the front door. Scott is emotionally healthy because he spent a significant amount of time working extremely hard to deal with his past hurts.

2. Believe it or not, being married to Scott is one of the easiest jobs in my life right now. I know marriage takes work, but smoothing out the kinks with him is easy because we've both already dealt with our baggage. Scott and I always attack the problem, and never each other. We look at the marriage as a work in progress.

3. Since Scott looks to the Lord to meet his every need, he is not disappointed when I fail him, but, instead, is thrilled when I join God in loving him. I find myself doing things for Scott out of love, and not out of obligation, because he puts no demands on me at all.

4. Scott lets me be me and never asks me to change for him. If Scott sees a weak area in me, he prays for me and entreats God to do the changing. He may mention it once, but after that he just prays.

5. Scott gives me foot rubs almost every night. I just had to throw that in!

6. Scott leaves me love notes all around the house.

7. He's not jealous of my successes or talents. He wants me to thrive and blossom and use my gifts to the fullest.

8. He sees into my heart. He thinks I'm beautiful no matter what weight I am. I know this because I gained seventy pounds the first year we were married. Part of the problem was going from the sunny climate of Los Angeles to the rainy climate in Oregon. Also, I didn't know anyone in Portland since I had no students yet. All I did was sit around eating bon bons and playing video games waiting for Scott to come home. During this time, my sole purpose in life was to cook big impressive meals for him. Though Scott was concerned for my health, he told me one night that he was actually glad I had gained the weight. He wanted me to be secure in the fact that he didn't love me because of external beauty. He wrote a song called "Gorgeous In, Gorgeous Out" for our wedding and I can't tell you how comforting it is to know that when I get old and wrinkly, Scott will still think I'm beautiful.

Now this is going to sound like a contradiction, but bear with me for a minute. Just when you think that all of the idols you cling to are taken care of, the Lord shows you another one. Darn that dross! Scott has been helping me see that food is an idol in my life. I turn to it when I feel insignificant.

I grew up in a family of ten where food disappeared quickly and treats barely made it out of the package. No wonder I occasionally discovered a box of Oreos stashed in my mom's dresser. Watching my dad eat Sara Lee cheesecake while the kids ate vanilla ice milk, left a lasting impression on me that eating the good stuff meant you were really important. Scott has helped me understand my unbalanced love affair with food. He is helping me successfully lose the weight and we celebrate every ten pounds lost.

9. Scott communicates. During the first year of our marriage we clashed on a few issues because of being older and somewhat set in our ways. The antidote?...Talking! We would literally take entire weekends, from Friday to Sunday night, to figure out a solution to the conflict. The rule was; it had to be a solution both of us could live with. Those long hours that we spent resolving our differences in the beginning stage of our marriage have certainly saved us a lot of time over the years! I know that most men don't like to talk, but my man gets grumpy if we haven't talked enough. I love that!

10. Scott is the spiritual leader in our home. He doesn't lord over me but shows me by example how to walk with God. I tell people all the time that Scott is the closest thing to a walking Jesus Christ I have ever met. (He hates when I say that too.) He moves with God. He hears from Him. It's so wonderful to be married to a man with a "direct line" to God. This connection really manifests itself when Scott decides he needs to change something in himself. Change doesn't come easily to him. But when he sees I am genuinely unhappy about a certain behavior, he prays about it. If God says it's a good change, then Scott sets out, in the power of the Holy Spirit, to change it. Now that's a lover leader.

~~~

Well, that's my list. Thirteen years living with the wrong guy felt like thirty. Seven years living with the right guy feels like an ongoing honeymoon. My heart still flutters when Scott walks in the door from work. Sometimes, when he's talking to me, I can't concentrate on what he's saying because in my mind I'm thinking, "Man, you are so cute! I want to kiss you right now!" Enough said.

All of this to say, Ladies, if you are looking for Mr. Right, let God do the matchmaking. You won't regret it. Trust me, I know because I tried it both ways. If you got it wrong the first time, and God, in His mercy, releases you, then let Him do it right for you the second time. After all...He is the God of second chances!

I'd like to end this book with a final reference to the last song on the CD called "The IOU Song" which is the latest one I've written to date. Seven years had passed since God and I wrote a tune. I'm not sure why such a long time had elapsed, but I think, maybe, it's because I've been so happy with Scott, that I haven't felt the need to get my innermost thoughts and emotions out.

About a month before my very first PJs Women's Conference, I said to the Lord, "We really need to write a closing 'thank you' song for this conference." But I was swamped trying to get the details done and didn't have a spare minute to write one. I would have used an old song from my repertoire, but I am ashamed to say that I have never written a song just thanking the Lord for everything He's done for me. How ungrateful is that!

Well, a few nights before the first conference, my eyes popped open at 4:00 am and the words "IOU song" came into my head. Then the Lord said, "Get up Kathy, we're going to write a song together."

I was so excited. This was the first song in seven years! With no arguments this time, I jumped out of bed and twenty minutes later, the song was done. God is so good. He knew I needed sleep so…"wham bam" and I was back in bed. Imagine the "God of this Universe"…my writing partner. How awesome! How humbling! I can't do a thing without Him. Thank you, Lord Jesus. I truly do owe you everything!

Track#18: IOU EVERYTHING

Verse 1
I owe you everything, everything.
My husband, my home, all that I own,
I owe it all to you, Lord.
Everything, everything.
What can I say? I could never repay
All that you've done for me.

Verse 2
I owe you everything, everything.
Each song that I sing, every gift that You bring,

I owe it all to you, Lord.
Everything…everything.
The skits and the skongs…they all belong,
They all belong to you.

Bridge
My Jesus I love Thee but that's not enough.
I've got to obey when the going gets rough.
I stop and complain at the first hint of pain.
Teach me to look at you…look at you.

Verse 3
You gave me everything, everything.
You suffered and died…"Forgive her!" You cried.
All so that I might live.
You are my everything, everything.
Let my heart be your home. I can't do this alone.
What can I give to repay what you did?
What can I say? I can never repay
All that you've done for me.
I owe you everything

So…that's my story. I hope that God has used it to bless your life and that you've enjoyed the ride.

The End

What is a PJs Women's Conference?

*K*athy Ashdown has found a way to combine several of her lifelong passions into one giant gift—Women's PJs Conferences. Having directed more than thirty musicals from L.A. to New York, she formed a production company called KFA productions. After teaching vocal students on Broadway as well as worship leaders from coast to coast, she developed a method of teaching by storytelling, drama and song that captivates and motivates her listeners. And finally, her love for the Lord and a deep desire to see women walk closely with Him through thick and thin are the driving forces behind her unique ministry to women.

She brings her production team with her. Her husband, Scott, is a well-known Christian psychologist; he provides professional guidance to those women who are especially hurting. With breakout sessions on subjects like, "How to have a Quiet Time in a Loud World," and "How to be Whole and Have Healthy Relationships," the weekend is both challenging and encouraging.

But the best thing about the weekend is the warm, cozy atmosphere with rest and relaxation a high priority. The women can actually stay in their jammies and sip hot chocolate from their favorite mug. The team even includes a professional reflexologist for foot rubs! If you would like a PJs Women's Conference at your church, please visit www.KathyAshdown.com

About the Authors

*K*athy and Dr. Scott Ashdown are the founders and directors of the PJs Women's Conference Weekends. They live in sunny Sarasota, Florida. Kathy has been teaching voice and piano for over thirty-five years and has directed over thirty musicals from L.A. to New York. She has been writing songs since she was ten years old and has just finished her first CD, "The God of Second Chances."

She was on the music ministry staff at The Grove Community Church in Los Angeles, California, and has led worship in churches all across the United States. She teaches women's Bible studies at Grace Baptist Church in Sarasota, Florida, and she also helps lead worship when she is not travelling.

Scott is a licensed psychologist with offices in Venice and Sarasota, Florida. He loves to teach on the side and has held the position of adjunct professor at George Fox University, Western Theological Seminary and Argosy University.

Dr. Scott had a previous career as a youth pastor and also spent ten years on the staff of Young Life. Scott received his Masters and Doctorate from George Fox University. He has made the integration of Christianity and psychology a major focus of his life, both professionally and personally. Scott speaks at the PJs Conferences and also meets with the women attending who are in crisis.

Kathy and Scott speak at women's events and church services throughout the country. If you would like to invite them to speak at your church, please visit www.KathyAshdown.com.

www.ingramcontent.com/pod-product-compliance
Lightning Source LLC
Chambersburg PA
CBHW051839090426
42736CB00011B/1888